CALL TO PURPOSE

CALL TO PURPOSE

How Men Make Sense of Life-Changing Experience

RICHARD SOLLY

 HAZELDEN®

Hazelden
Center City, Minnesota 55012-0176

Library of Congress Cataloging-in-Publication Data
Solly, Richard.
    Call to purpose: how men make sense of life-changing
experience/Richard Solly.
        p.   cm.
    Includes bibliographical references (p.).
    ISBN 1-56838-045-3: $11.95 ($17.95 Can.)
    1. Men—Religious life. 2. Experience (Religion). 3. Life change
events—Religious aspects.   I. Title.
BL625.65.S65   1995
291.4'2'081—dc20
                                                            94-46389
                                                                CIP

Editor's note
Hazelden offers a variety of information on chemical dependency
and related areas. Our publications do not necessarily represent
Hazelden's programs, nor do they officially speak for any Twelve Step
organization.

In Memory of
My Father, Mother, and Sister:
Ladimar, Rose, and Louise Solly

*A man may go for many years
with an inkling of something,
but grasps it clearly only at
a particular moment.*
— Carl Jung

CONTENTS

.

ACKNOWLEDGMENTS

No book is without a stage crew that works behind the scenes in bringing it to its audience. John Small and Terry Spohn are certainly members of that crew. I thank them for their enthusiastic response to my idea for a book on sacred moments and men's spirituality. I'm indebted to my good friend author Cheri Register for the long hours she put in on this book. She tirelessly labored on each chapter, reading drafts and suggesting revisions. Her knowledge and experience helped enlarge the scope of this book, and I could always count on her support and encouragement. I also owe a great deal to my daughter, Rosie, an inspiration and blessing in my life. I also thank those men and women whose interviews and stories do not appear in this book, but who contributed largely to the premises and conclusions I reached. Finally, I am grateful to the men in this book for opening their hearts and souls, giving us all a glimpse of their sacred moments.

INTRODUCTION

Weeks before spring, when crocuses, apple trees, tulips, lilac bushes, and pink columbine were ready to blossom, I lay in a hospital bed tangled in a web of intravenous tubes. An abdominal infection had spread to every part of my body, including my blood. I had septicemia, or blood poisoning, and went into shock as my blood pressure plummeted to sixty over zero.

Twice during that time, my deceased father and sister appeared at the foot of my bed. Both were typically dressed: he in a white shirt with rolled up sleeves and dress trousers, and she in a yellow nightgown with a white lace collar that I remembered her wearing during her long illness. Only my father spoke, assuring me, "If you cross over, we'll meet you." That was my second near-death experience. Weeks earlier, with a lung infection, I had floated up off my bed into a brilliant white room with no door and had felt a profound bliss.

After my discharge from the hospital I hesitated to speak to even my friends about the psychological, social, and spiritual upheaval I was in. I felt vulnerable to any remark that might minimize what had happened to me. Six months later I cautiously disclosed the events to my family doctor, who suggested I read about near-death experiences.

Many of the books I read left me dissatisfied. Rather than focus on the various meanings near-death perceptions held for individuals, the books seemed pseudoscientific as they sought to argue for the reality and accuracy of such perceptions. I didn't need anyone to argue on my behalf. I wanted to read a book that focused on people's struggle to interpret and integrate the meanings these sacred moments held for their everyday lives, regardless of whether anyone else thought the visions were real or hallucinatory. I felt that authors who argued that people's visions and revelations proved the existence of an afterlife, a God, or even a more secular supraconsciousness failed to understand that no argument, no matter how persuasive, would eliminate the need for faith. Again, I didn't need proof. I needed encouragement and support in transforming my life along the ethical lines which my experiences in the hospital demanded. Some people might turn to religious leaders for that support, but for me, a former Catholic, it wasn't at hand.

I began asking friends if they had ever experienced a moment in their lives which affected them so profoundly that they might call it spiritual or religious. I was startled by how many people had, and how many, like me, kept silent about these moments for fear of being regarded as lunatics or religious fanatics. One person referred me to another, and in time I interviewed many people from different backgrounds with "varieties of religious experiences," some of which are shared in this book.

Initially, I interviewed both men and women. However, I found the men's interviews more dramatic and surprising because I had not expected them to talk so openly about their suffering and vulnerability. They also raised distinct questions about the impact of their newfound spirituality on their perceptions of themselves as men. I decided that there was a need at this time for a book that focused on the state of men's spirituality.

Honored to have such a deep look into men's souls, I still wondered how fruitful discussing spirituality along gender lines would be. Women had been doing just that, but surely the plethora of books on women's spirituality results more from their protest against being excluded from the male hierarchy of religious institutions than from any ontological differences between the sexes.

Perhaps different solutions, myths, and resources may be more appealing and pertinent just now for each sex. It may be necessary to extenuate the division of God into Father and Mother, symbols of sky and earth, concepts like Yin and Yang, myths like Prometheus and Demeter or Adam and Eve, and even deeper polarities before we can experience the Whole. Maybe God must be divided into masculine and feminine, not for the purpose of conquest, but to restore wholeness; but we must first acknowledge, accept, and love the divisions. As the poet Robert Bly has said, "It's important to be able to say the word masculine without imagining that we are saying a sexist word." Until we can, we have not only lost God as Mother, but also as the kind of Father we long for. The image of the male parent in our society as absent, punishing, selfish, abusive, insensitive, and stupid inevitably discolors the image of God as Father, making him inadequate for these men also.

Gender roles significantly affect how men and women approach their spirituality. Because of the taboos against intimacy and vulnerability, men are traditionally reluctant to talk about their personal faith and emotional experiences. Conventional wisdom says that men often talk to each other about sex by bragging, but even bragging isn't likely to be used to talk about spirituality. While men study theology and pursue careers as clergymen, they tend to shy away from discussion of personal piety, which is what the sacred moment awakes. It appears "as if mysticism were for saintly women and theological study for practical but, alas, unsaintly men," says Thomas Merton. Of course, there are exceptions like pious fundamentalists.

The central questions I sought to answer in conducting these interviews were: What do men *do* with their experiences of the sacred? Where do they go to discuss their sacred moments? How do they determine the meaning that the sacred moment will have for their lives? What choices do they make in living out their revitalized spirituality? How do they integrate their personal experience of the Divine into their outlook on life and the habits they live by?

This book doesn't offer any obvious answers, but it does offer the stories of eight men who have had life-changing experiences that deepened their spiritual lives. They represent various professions, ages, geographies, and religious backgrounds from Protestant, Catholic, and Jewish. Each of the stories shows a man coping with suffering, which is common to all of us. They endure and are transformed by the deaths of loved ones, injury from accidents, illness, divorce, disability, or troubled consciences. Their sacred moments have helped shape a vital, spiritual life in the world. The stories let us look into the smithy of a man's soul, forged by suffering and tempered by the sacred. As poet Yehuda Amichai writes, "through the wound in my chest God peers into the universe." It is through the wounds in these men, their defeats and victories, their sorrows and joys that we get a glimpse of God.

CHAPTER 1

Making Sense of a Spiritual Life

The sacred is not so much a building or an institution as an event, something that happens.

—Dorothee Soelle

When I began interviewing for this book, I immediately encountered some serious difficulty with terminology. Some men adamantly refused to call their experience "religious" and insisted on the term "spiritual." Others used the terms interchangeably. At first, I thought this distinction in language might divide the men neatly into those who were actively religious and those who weren't. If the use of "religious" or "spiritual" depended only on whether someone went to a church or synagogue, it seemed artificial. Did a man have to practice his spiritual beliefs within an established religion to have his sacred moment validated as a religious experience? On the other hand, didn't traditionally religious men have a spiritual dimension to their lives? Was there really a critical difference between the spiritual and the religious?

In 1902, William James, psychologist and philosopher, used the words "religious experience" in his book *The Varieties of Religious Experience* to describe the event that I have chosen to call a "sacred moment." However, he defined the term not along the lines of religious dogma or theology, but as "feelings, acts, and experiences of individual men in their solitude, so far as they apprehend themselves to stand in relation to whatever they may consider the divine."

His definition is especially helpful at resolving the confusion between "religious" and "spiritual." Though he distinguishes personal experience from theory or theology, he nevertheless perceives the soul and psyche as one. Though many of the men I interviewed experienced their personal faith and religious practices as distinctly separate, James' definition points the way to a more appreciative and holistic approach to religious experiences or sacred moments.

In 1935, the problem with the terms "religious" and "spiritual" came sharply into focus again when Bill Wilson, cofounder of Alcoholics Anonymous

(AA), described the new Twelve Step program as "spiritual rather than religious." Though he partly derived this revolutionary statement from his readings of William James, Wilson drew a sharp line between the terms. Separating the spiritual from the religious enabled him to bring nonreligious alcoholics—atheists, agnostics—together with alcoholics who had strong religious roots to talk about their common struggle. Wilson's statement also eased the minds of clergy who were afraid the AA program might usurp their roles or lead alcoholics in their congregations astray.

Today, the word "spiritual" has been picked up by the New Age movement, which makes some mainstream religious denominations wary. Some theologians may avoid the term "spiritual," thinking it suggests the occult and superstition rather than religious faith. The word "spirituality" is preferred by other clergy who want to make religion more palatable to those who feel restricted by doctrine and authority. Some accept the distinction between spiritual and religious and try to define the words more clearly. One lay person may use the term to mean personal piety, while another uses it as a defense. When asked if he is religious, he replies, "No, I'm not religious, but I'm spiritual." This distinction enables him to claim an identity apart from "churchy" people and practices he may see as rigid or hypocritical, yet affirms his own quest for the

Divine or Transcendent. Many others perceive little difference between the terms "spiritual" and "religious."

I use the terms interchangeably. I have no difficulty calling an agnostic's sacred moment a religious experience. The etymology of the word "religion" makes no reference to a man's belief system. The word has two Latin sources, and the first refers to a state or "bond between man and the gods." The second emphasizes purpose or action, "to bind." Both definitions concern the primal relationship between man and God, not what church he attends or what theology he espouses. Whether a man is a churchgoer or not, during a sacred moment he is bound to a divinity or power beyond himself. We need to be tolerant and see that religious people have genuine spiritual lives and that many nonreligious people who have no formal affiliation nevertheless accept traditional religious doctrines. Most importantly, what matters is not what we call the sacred moment, but what it means for the man experiencing the holy.

Jewish and Christian scriptures contain many profound examples of the sacred moment: Abraham's covenant, Joseph's wrestling match with the Angel, Moses' encounter with the burning bush, Mary's Annunciation, the women's meeting with the risen Christ, and Paul's conversion on the road to Damascus. In other religious traditions, people expect holy men and women, shamans with direct experiences of God, to take leadership roles in their societies. Until science and reason gained hegemony as superior routes to the truth, spiritual experiences in the Western world had a valued place and meaning in everyday life. Revelations and visions of the divine were commonly reported. Men as different as Martin Luther and St. John of the Cross reported intense experiences of God and the Divine. Dreams of the holy and sacred moments were nothing to scoff at. People like John Calvin, St. Ignatius, and St. Theresa trusted their experiences of God and contributed to forming the spiritual life of their societies along the lines of their personal visions.

Of course, there is a strong and continuing tradition of men, like Thomas Merton or Matthew Fox, who turn inward for light. But even in the religious contemplative tradition—among Trappist monks, for example—the expectation is that these men will leave the day-to-day world and devote themselves to prayer and study as a vocation. But what choices do ordinary men have to pursue spiritual matters in their daily lives in the secular world? What will they do? Where do they go to discuss their spiritual identities and personal piety?

Men who are affiliated with a religious institution would presumably turn to their church or synagogue for help in understanding the sacred moment and its meaning for their lives. Yet many do not do so. The way in which their accounts of a personal religious experience are received by their clergy may depend greatly on how their denominations view the individuals' relationship to God, as well as on the forms of knowledge their denominations value most highly. Today the meaning a particular Christian Church makes of the sacred moment depends greatly on the relative importance it assigns to what Presbyterian minister John Ackerman calls experience, tradition, or scripture.

Some Pentecostal or Evangelical churches that highly value experience may welcome a personal account of a meeting with God, yet demand that its truth be demonstrated by a certain prescribed behavior, such as witnessing to others who are not yet "saved." In the Catholic church, which emphasizes tradition and theology, a man may find that his enthusiasm to testify about experiencing God in the woods or seeing God in an orange embarrasses or worries his fellow parishioners. Some Protestant denominations, suspicious of pietism, may give priority to scriptural rather than experiential truth. I have wondered how likely it is for a man to have his story validated just as he experienced it, without either skepticism or preconceived notions of how it ought to change his life.

During the course of writing this book, I came to believe that men who were not churchgoers, those without support from clergy, community, dogma, or creeds, were uniquely challenged to make sense of their spiritual lives. In their sacred moments they seemed most alone. Though they were no less devout or pious, their visions and revelations were not easily assimilated and usually required years of effort. In their struggle to articulate the ineffable without using traditional religious language and imagery, they were often frustrated.

I also believed for a time that more credibility might be gained for the spiritual experience if I focused on the nonreligious. No one, I thought, would find these people fanatical because they had no axe to grind; and no one would misread my book as an effort to proselytize. The reader could trust these people as particularly convincing witnesses of the Divine. Many of the men I interviewed were agnostic at different times in their lives, and one man remained so. Their attitudes towards church and religion ranged from hostility and apathy to extensive involvement. Many just couldn't find enough energy or interest to attend religious services. Though they valued the religious spirit, they remained outside the church or synagogue, uncertain whether they were going to step inside or away for good. Many of them are similar to people described by Howard Rice in his book *Reformed Spirituality* as "believing without belonging."

I found the uncertainty of these people testifying to a kind of faith. Because they recognized a value and truth in all religions, including Eastern philosophies and Native American rituals and myths, they found it difficult to commit to any one in particular. Some men stood on the doorstep, not in protest, but torn between wanting in and wanting out. Their desire to belong to a religious community conflicted with their need to maintain personal integrity. Others suffered no conflict but stood on the doorstep out of choice. Their commitment to such traditional religious values as honesty, humility, charity, prayer, and nonviolence was as exemplary as that of many within the church.

Whether the man was nondenominational or belonged to a formal religion, his sacred moment affected him dramatically. However, these men did not suddenly sprout wings and fly off like angels. They were transformed, but rarely in as striking a manner as St. Paul. No one reported having finally arrived at Nirvana or unification where all things merged. In fact, many repressed the spiritual experience only to have it affect them years later.

Though people's sacred moments took place "in their solitude" and were at first kept secret, they did not isolate the men but eventually connected them more deeply to humanity, the cosmos, the community, religion, or to the Other. What was discovered in solitude always created union, connecting people to something or someone greater than themselves. The sacred wasn't an object like a relic or icon in a church, but rather always a subject, an experience in the everyday world. What these men called divine always grounded them in humility and reverence for *this* world.

In each of the men's sacred moments, I found commonalities. Though they are more fully discussed in chapter 8, I want to introduce the reader to them here. The seven qualities of the sacred moment are: brevity, unexpectedness, ineffability, ordinary setting, union with a transcendent Being, vivid recall of details, and most importantly, an enduring, transformational effect. Unpredictable, the men's experiences occurred in unlikely settings, such as in a man's kitchen, on a street, or in the woods. Readers will find some sacred moments lasting only as long as one man can hold his breath. The men spoke of being in the presence of "something or someone" or having a heightened consciousness identified as transcendent. The details of the everyday world, the skin of an orange or the shape of snowflakes, were more vivid and sensual than the men had normally experienced. Most importantly, each sacred moment had a transformational effect on the men, illustrating the "fruit" by which their sacred moments can be judged efficacious and wholesome.

CHAPTER 2

A Clearing in the Woods

For nothing is secret that shall not be made manifest.

—Luke 8:17

The alarm in the cabin rang at three in the morning that early fall day in Northern Minnesota. Greg, who was twenty years old then, his father and two brothers, a cousin, and an uncle woke and quickly dressed. They fried eggs and bacon for breakfast, then packed additional food, cartridges, and a change of socks in their backpacks. Slinging rifles over their shoulders, they left the cabin to position themselves before daybreak.

The four young men and their fathers followed a dirt road, grooved with deep tire tracks, to a spot marked the day before with a piece of cloth at the edge of the woods. Twigs snapped under their boots as they stepped off the road into pine and birch trees. As they talked, they could see their breath. When the hunting group found the ideal location, Greg unfolded the deer stand he carried and inserted the v-shaped strut into the tree. He fastened the stand's belt around the trunk, ten to fifteen feet off the ground to shield the hunter from the keen eyes and nose of the deer. Greg then shimmied up the tree and positioned himself on the stand.

As the sun rose and darkness left the woods, Greg peered steadily into the trees. He heard crows and leaves rustling. Believing a deer was about to step out from behind a copse of bushes, he hoisted his gun to his shoulder and aimed. When he saw a rabbit scurry out from under the bush, he lowered his rifle.

The two fathers were skillful hunters, but Greg had never shot a deer. As he sat in the stand, he fantasized about being the only one in the hunting party to shoot one. He imagined sighting a buck only thirty yards from him, lifting his gun and taking aim. As the gun shot rang out in the woods and the deer fell, he would holler, "I got him!" Others in the hunting party would run to him, congratulating him on his kill. But no sooner had his fantasy ended did Greg recall his friend Bill, whom he met while they both were studying for the priesthood at a seminary prep school. He recalled the many nights they stayed up, discussing the immorality of killing and the Vietnam war. As Greg looked out into woods, he suddenly felt guilty about hunting deer, as if he were betraying his friend. Now the thought of sighting one in the scope of his gun, squeezing the trigger, and watching the animal tumble to the ground as the bullet ripped into its side troubled him.

The sound of crackling twigs alerted Greg. Something or someone was coming through the trees behind him, and as he turned he lifted his gun from his lap. When he spotted the orange hunter's jacket between two bushes, he sighed and lowered his rifle. It was his father. As he came closer and waved, Greg, looking down from the deer stand, noticed how much smaller his father seemed. Greg had always thought of him as a large, burly man, but at that moment his father, standing below him, seemed little and frail.

"Here," his father said, handing his son a silver flask of blackberry brandy. Greg reached down and took the flask. Greg was legally under the drinking age, but it was as if his father were saying, "Here, take a swig, you're a man now." Greg lifted the flask to his mouth and swigged. The sweet warm taste was soothing. "Go ahead," his father said. "Take another."

Greg drank again from the flask and handed it back down. His father wiped its mouth with a gloved hand and swigged. Greg knew that in a couple of hours of sipping brandy his father would grow more oblivious of the cold and sit quietly in his deer stand until his brother came to get him.

Greg stared out into the woods. "Spot anything?" his father asked.

"No. I heard something earlier, but it was only a rabbit." Nothing more was said while Greg and his father gazed through the trees. Greg considered talking to his father about why he left seminary school for a pre-med program at the university. But he knew the subject would only disturb his father, disappointed in Greg for not becoming a priest. Because their hometown doctor was so admired by their family, Greg had thought a pre-med program would win his father's approval as had his theological studies, but it hadn't. With seven siblings, Greg's academic decisions were based primarily on getting his parents' approval rather than on any passionate desire to become a priest or doctor. Science and math classes were equally discouraging for Greg. Days before the hunting trip he had felt especially disillusioned. He wanted to take a year off from his studies, but the prospect of being drafted and sent to Vietnam while out of school worried him.

"Well, I better get back before some buck wanders over to my tree," his father joked before leaving.

Greg had looked forward to the hunting trip, an escape from city traffic and noise. Spending time in the woods with his father and brothers would be a reprieve from his arduous studies at the university. But as he watched his father trek back through the woods to his stand, Greg felt regretful and discouraged. Now he wished he hadn't come on the hunting trip. What a waste of time, he thought, shivering all day in a deer stand, talking to no one. His lips were chapped and burned by the wind.

After nearly six hours in the stand, Greg had not sighted a single deer. His feet and hands were cold and numb; his joints stiffened. He was bored and unhappy. "I've had it," he said out loud to himself. He shimmied back down from his stand, slung his rifle over his shoulder, and followed a trail in the snow back to his father's stand. "I'm going back to the cabin," he told him.

The cabin was over a mile away from where his father was positioned. As Greg made his way back through the woods, stepping over tree roots and fallen limbs, he felt dejected. He had not fired a single shot, let alone spotted a deer. Now, he wasn't even sure if he would have fired if he had spotted one. As he plodded along, cradling his rifle, he could see a clearing twenty yards ahead.

"I remember it exactly," he said. "It had a slight rise to it and was circular, surrounded by tall birch trees. The white peeling bark now seemed more vivid. A path, probably made by deer, cut straight across the clearing." At first, Greg felt strangely apprehensive because walking out into the open left him exposed and vulnerable, but as he stepped out of the trees into the clearing he was suddenly struck by how beautiful it was. "It had just started to snow," he said. "At first the flakes were small, but then huge snowflakes began coming down, in slow motion! And then the size of the snowflakes changed and became more regular, but they were strangely equidistant from each other. I remember that. Each snowflake was perfect. This is difficult to explain but it felt like something was coming down in the snow. A Presence. I was awestruck and I just stood there. I held the rifle and watched snowflakes fall on the gun barrel. I wondered if they would rust the metal. I wasn't cold any longer, and I remember just wanting to stand there. I felt a presence of God, and I was overwhelmed by it. I wasn't able to make a choice about walking through the clearing right away or not. All I could do was stand there and take it in. Tears came to my eyes. All sorts of things were going through me.

"I had a sense of healing going on there," Greg added, "but this is hard to explain now. Standing in that clearing, I was somehow receiving reassurance that I wasn't alone. There was a power outside myself that was immensely stronger than me. Everything was going to be okay: my worries about school, Vietnam, and my career choices and decisions. I felt connected to people before me—I mean hundreds of years before me—and I thought of early American Indians, how this would happen to them in the woods. The word 'majestic' comes to mind to explain what happened."

Standing in awe as the snow fell, Greg's rare and brief moment before the Presence might have made him exclaim, "Aha! Now I see!" But even those words couldn't describe his bliss. He felt connected to the universe, nature, and God—having an unutterable sense of oneness, assurance, and clarity. Who would dare utter a word or do anything? His sudden, altered consciousness of something immensely stronger and majestic was similar to what William James described as a "feeling of objective presence...'something there.'"

Greg's serendipitous discovery of "something" in the clearing, falling in the snow, afloat in perfectly shaped snowflakes, was nothing he had even thought of seeking. He felt physically transported, lifted out of the ordinary woods where he was hunting and set down into a forest of bliss. Now, with a new vision, he saw the whiteness of snow, peeling bark, and "perfect" snowflakes as he had never seen them before. In the clearing, his body felt as airy and afloat as the snow, "at one with nature." Though his sacred moment in the woods lasted only "ten or fifteen minutes," in some inexplicable way for Greg it seemed to last forever.

He recalled how his mystical connection to his

ancestors and the Presence slowly dissipated. Once again, he began to feel cold and tired. The gun grew heavy, and his legs and back ached from standing still for so long. "The clearing began to drain of the Presence and look ordinary. The snow thinned out to tiny crystals and sunlight poured down between the tree tops. I knew it was necessary to continue on, to let go of the ecstasy. As I walked, I promised myself to come back to this spot. I'd tell no one; it could be my special place."

When he finally reached the cabin, he was met by his cousin who talked excitedly about his killing of a young buck. "I remember suddenly feeling dread," Greg said.

When the other men returned and stood on the cabin porch, pounding their feet to clean the mud off their boots, Greg did not rush outside to tell them of his religious experience. He would have liked to fling open the cabin door and announce on the porch that he had experienced God, but acutely aware of how foolish he might sound, he kept silent. He could not easily dismiss the rational arguments of his own mind that argued against his experience. Afraid of being ridiculed, Greg never mentioned his sacred moment in the woods to anyone in the hunting party.

For the rest of the evening in the cabin, he questioned himself. Perhaps his awareness of a divine Presence was a mental aberration, resulting from exhaustion and sensory deprivation from hours of sitting in a deer stand. Perhaps two swigs of brandy was more than he could handle. He imagined Father O'Connor from the seminary cautioning him about an overactive imagination and encouraging him to return to the seminary. He knew what his cousin would say. Had Greg told him, he would have calmly and rationally informed Greg that the reassurance he felt coming from a greater power was *merely* personal and subjective. It proved nothing about the existence of God, but only how fatigued Greg was. Greg even imagined his seminary friend calling his peak experience profound reverie, not a spiritual experience of God.

After supper, the men lit a fire in the fireplace and gathered chairs in front of it. The topic of discussion remained hunting. Greg was quiet, feeling the heat of the fire on his face and listening to crackling flames. "I'm just tired," he said when questioned about his silence. He excused himself and retired to bed early.

That evening, if he could have recalled reading William James in seminary school, he might have remembered that the individual's experience was "the real backbone of the world's religious life." No argument his cousin might have made, nor any dogma at seminary school, could have weakened the spine of Greg's own spiritual life. He might have drawn reassurance and support for his experience, and rested peacefully, instead of tossing in bed. He might have said then what he would say twenty years later. "It doesn't matter, because I believe; I know."

The next morning, while his father prepared breakfast, Greg left the cabin and began walking back through the woods, hoping to find the clearing. Because of snowfall the night before, he was unable to locate the exact spot. "I think I walked back on that path, but it was disappointing. Though I didn't have the turmoil about Vietnam and class work from the day before, I felt a little sad."

Still, the few minutes Greg stood in the clearing the day before were as real to him as the hours he spent in the deer stand. That morning, no one could convince him that what he saw and felt in his body was any less real because of its spiritual nature. From that day forward, "The moment anchored in me a belief in God and became a point of reference in my spiritual life," he said.

Greg wanted to tell someone about the Presence in the clearing, yet powerful social forces silenced him. He felt vulnerable because his experience was so personal and intimate and he could not trust himself to talk about it. He kept his sacred moment secret for so long that in time he began to question the reliability of his own memory.

Though secrecy and silence have long been associated with religious cults and rituals, Greg had another, apparently more mundane reason for keeping silent. He tried once, during his last year of undergraduate school, to tell a friend about what he witnessed in the woods. But he felt frustrated and discouraged by how superficial and trite he sounded. His friend simply nodded and said, "Oh." He realized then that he was only communicating the words and not the experience, which remained for him ineffable and beyond description. The truths of his sacred moment couldn't be communicated without the experience itself. "There can be no depth without the way to the depth," theologian Paul Tillich wrote. "Truth without the way to truth is dead; if it still be used, it contributes only to the surface of things."

Greg's friend was only hearing "the surface" while the "depth" remained hidden. Afterwards, Greg vowed again not to speak about his sacred moment. Silence had both positive and negative repercussions for him. It guarded his sacred moment from being diminished, yet kept him from coming to terms with it.

"I never spoke again about my experience to anyone until fifteen years later," Greg said. When he did, it was only once, in a relaxation course where he was urged to visualize a tranquil scene from his past. Though he described the physical clearing to others in the course, he never disclosed the landscape of his soul in that clearing. He avoided mentioning the spiritual and intimate details of his experience. His reluctance partly resulted from a conflict over spirituality and religion, between God and himself.

"To discuss what happened to me in the woods, I would have had to come to terms with God," Greg said. "I would have had to put the experience into a context and that context probably would have had to be religious. I couldn't express it that way. As soon as it would have been verbalized, negative emotions would have come up. It took me a long time to see it was okay to have a spiritual life.

"I think men's spirituality is lived internally, but it is clandestine," Greg says today. Recalling a New Testament passage, he added, "Men shouldn't hide their candles under baskets." Jesus had warned his disciples not to hide their candles under bushels, but to put them on candlesticks so that they might give others light. Jesus' warning makes clear that the light of a man's spiritual life shouldn't remain secret or underground, but be revealed in appropriate settings. If a man made no effort to take his soul out into the world where others could see it, the efficacy of his spiritual moment could wane and darken, go even deeper into hiding, and be lost to himself.

The longer Greg kept silent, the more the light of his Epiphany dimmed in his consciousness until he grew suspicious of his own memory. His reluctance to talk to anyone about his sacred moment further suppressed his conflict with the spiritual. As a consequence, he wasn't able to move ahead in his spiritual life. Telling someone about the spiritual event in the clearing might have brought the oxygen his sacred moment needed to flame brightly.

In part, Greg's self-doubt was intensified because he didn't understand that his experience was far more prevalent in American society than he imagined. He thought sacred moments were the exclusive property of mystics or even madmen. Sacred moments, like his, were assigned by Divine Providence to a few special individuals for their outstanding virtue.

Today, Greg realizes that people like himself who claim to have a vision or experience of God or a Transcendent are not claiming special status. "I think many people have awarenesses like mine," Greg added. "Mine connected me to the human experience. Though it links me directly to God, it doesn't elevate me above others or make me more advanced. The more I advance in my spirituality, the more common I become—like a servant to others, in service. The need to compare myself to others diminishes as my spirituality evolves, and I focus on accepting the nature of things, like how incomplete I am, my shortcomings, the injustices, pain in the world, senseless things. I'm responsible for taking care of myself, but I help others by volunteering my services."

Greg is not a mystical type steeped in introspection and seclusion. Raised as a Catholic, he drifted away from the church. He abandoned his studies in pre-med as well as in theology, and by the age of forty-three, he was working in the Midwest as a maintenance supervisor and caretaker of a barrier-free living apartment unit for the disabled and seniors. He also received income as a personal care attendant for one of the residents. He is a divorced father of two children whom he sees every other weekend. His more typical male activities involve fishing, browsing through hardware stores, and making home repairs. He can often be found painting a living room, moving appliances and furniture, or doing general plumbing and electrical work.

In the last year, Greg has been attending a liberal Catholic church. He will soon finish his graduate studies in counseling psychology. He talked about the role his sacred moment continues to play in motivating his return to school.

"My spiritual experience confirmed in me that human relations are more important than the acquisition of things and profit-making. It tells me who I am, and it made helping others okay. People come first. That's why I'm shifting from the business world of property management to counseling. The difficult part is ignoring old messages about where I ought to be."

A few years after his experience in the woods,

Greg went hunting again with a group of men. Rather than lug a deer stand and gun through the woods, he took only a camera which allowed him to be with the others without violating his values. He described another recent hunting trip which he preferred to call a retreat in the woods with one of his sons, his brother, and his brother's son. It did not strike Greg until the interview that the situation of two brothers with their children was exactly the one he had been in twenty years earlier. This time, Greg was the father taking his own fourteen-year-old son into the woods.

Greg felt he responded to his own son much differently than his father had responded to him. "I'm more verbal and talk to my son a lot. My father wasn't that way. We spent time together and stayed in the same cabin. We all took a sauna together. I wouldn't have done that with my father. I never shot the gun. My son didn't bring one at all. He stayed in the cabin, read, slept in late. For us, it was alone time in the woods."

Though there are other activities, such as fishing, which Greg enjoys with his family, hunting still lures him back into the woods with other men and his two sons. Despite the hunting trip in his early twenties, he still associates hunting and nature with mythical qualities and male companionship. He feels something special can exist between a father and son in the woods. This myth has passed from one generation to another. The hours Greg may spend peering through the trees, gazing up at the sky on a chilly autumn morning, listening to twigs snap and leaves rustle are rewarding enough. A shot doesn't need to be fired. Just to spot a deer hopping over a fallen tree trunk is enough to delight him. These days in the woods give his life a depth and immeasurable quality.

The sense of a Presence in nature never left Greg, and today he vividly recalls the size of the snowflakes, the narrow path across the clearing, and the Spirit in the snow. He needs no proof, photograph, or imprimatur to authenticate his religious experience. On a weekend, he will suddenly decide to drive north towards the lakes and forests. He often finds, not the exact clearing where he once stood before God, but space and peace to be with himself, with his sons or other men. Alongside a lake, on a path, or in another clearing in the woods, he may look out, remember, and again stand still, in awe.

CHAPTER 3

The Prayer inside the Box

Maybe you did not hear it. But certainly it was spoken to you. For there is always a word from the Lord, a word that has been spoken.
— Paul Tillich

It was March 1958 when Larry Kegan stood on the breakwater wall in his swimsuit. Gulls flew over him, shrieking as their white bodies rose and fell on wind currents. He gazed out across an ocean studded with jeweled sunlight that windy morning in Miami Beach where he was vacationing with his family. It was the first time Larry, not yet sixteen years old, ever stood alone facing the ocean.

Larry's trip to Florida was partly intended by his father as a reward for Larry's good behavior while on a year's probation after being arrested with another youth for car theft. His father, a retired Navy officer, had transferred Larry from the high school he was attending to a military school to keep him from being expelled for incorrigibility. His father hoped military school would discipline and shape Larry into a "real man." However, soon after he began school, he was arrested after a high speed chase in a stolen car.

For Larry that afternoon on the breakwall, the blue sky, streaked with white, sloping down to the horizon seemed unreal. Waves slammed against the stone wall. He felt anxious as he bent his knees, preparing to jump feet-first twenty feet down into the water.

"Don't jump! Dive like I did!" hollered Tim, a twenty-one-year-old man Larry had met a week earlier at the hotel, who was bobbing in the waves. "You can do it!" Tim yelled again.

He gestured to his friend in the water. If Tim can do it, so can I, Larry thought. What he didn't know was that the waves crashing high against the breakwater wall left a trough of shallow water only a few feet deep in their wake. Tim, a more experienced swimmer from California, knew how to dive safely into the crest of a seven foot wave by timing his jump perfectly, landing on his belly, and riding the wave out to deeper water.

Larry crouched, leaned, pushed himself off the wall, and dove headfirst into the water. A large wave had already hit the wall and was flowing back out. Larry plunged into the shallow trough of water and struck his head on the bottom. Instantly paralyzed from a fractured neck and a damaged spinal cord, he lay in the water face down in a dead man's float, buffeted by waves. He did not lose consciousness. In shock, he couldn't grasp the enormous meaning of the pain he felt in his head. Larry tried lifting his head out of the water to take a breath, but couldn't. His mind and body were no longer one, but disconnected and unrelated, as if they existed in separate worlds. Larry knew something was seriously wrong. "I realized the rest of my life was going to last as long as I could hold my breath," he said.

His chest tightened to hold the air left in his lungs. In the few minutes remaining, he bobbed on waves like driftwood. It made no difference that less than three feet below him was the sandy ocean bottom covered with beautiful shells. Whether in three feet or twenty feet, he only needed a mouthful of water to drown.

Phantasmagoric images from his past suddenly flashed before him as if he were viewing a film underwater. "My life was going before me like a slide show," he said. "I saw the first girl I ever made love with. I was dancing with her, hugging her as tight as I possibly could." Her body, pressed against his, was as real and sensual under the water as it had been when they were both fourteen.

In the ocean, Larry smelled her perfume and saw other girls dancing in poodle skirts with heavy crinoline slips worn under them. A record of Teresa Brewer singing "Momma Don't Cry at My Wedding" was playing. There was no difference between then and now, between what was and what is. For Larry, time as he knew it had stopped. The past and present mingled in the waves. He had no sooner kissed his date, when "I suddenly saw myself wearing a red sleeveless cardigan sweater with a white shirt and black pants, singing on stage at a high school dance with three other young men. Emblems on the sweaters read 'The Jokers,' the name of our doo-wop harmonizing band."

As Larry's life passed before his eyes, he felt as if he existed everywhere, all at once. He saw a 1953 Chevy convertible suspended and floating in the water just as he was. "It had a continental kit—it was the car I stole," he said. No one could have guessed that he would relive the high-speed car chase that led to his arrest, not in a dream as he slept in a comfortable bed at a Florida resort, but floating face down in the water.

Larry's life review abruptly changed from the chase to a classroom at Mount Zion Temple where, upon the insistence of his grandparents, immigrants from a shtetl, a Jewish village in Ukraine, he received religious instruction in a Hebrew school every Saturday. With thirty other boys, he sat in the room, slouched in his chair. He was watching a film about the Holocaust, which seemed actually present to him in the water.

Larry was visibly disturbed by the sight of emaciated Jews herded into gas chambers. "I never saw so many sad faces walking to their death," he said, explaining his astonishment to the Rabbi that Saturday. Larry heard the people in the film chanting something undecipherable and asked what they were saying. The Rabbi explained that they were reciting the Shema prayer in Hebrew, "the holiest and highest of all prayers," which begins "Hear O Israel, Lord Our God, The Lord is One."

"What's so important about that prayer?" Larry asked the Rabbi.

"If you say that prayer before you die, you'll go to a very good place," the Rabbi explained. Larry had an impression of an afterlife, some place eternal.

As Larry bobbed in the ocean about to gulp a fatal mouthful of water, "something or someone told me to say the Shema prayer," the only Hebrew words he remembered.

He didn't know what or who the "something or someone" was. It was more than just a voice, but a presence that filled the water and his body. Did the voice belong to God? Was it a hallucination caused by oxygen deprivation and the buildup of carbon dioxide in his blood cells? Or had his grandmother who died a few months earlier intervened now on his behalf?

Larry could only be certain that when he said, "Hear O Israel, Lord Our God . . ." his life review ended. Suddenly, back on the breakwater wall, he was looking down at himself, a lifeless heap of bones in the water. "I didn't want to go back into my body, but a voice above me said: 'it's not time yet.'

"The next thing I knew, there was a warm, hot light hitting my face. I could hear my breathing but I couldn't feel anything. My head felt disconnected from my body, but I felt the sun on my face."

Tim, who first thought Larry was only feigning injury, finally realized the seriousness of the situation and swam back to him. He had turned Larry over, face up, so he could breathe. Larry opened his eyes, saw the bright sun in the blue sky. As he gasped for air, he suddenly returned to his body. Tim held his hand under Larry's head as a parent might cradle a baby and carefully eased him through the water to the shore.

Throughout the ordeal, Larry never went unconscious. As the ambulance speeded with its siren blaring down the very highway he drove the night before in Tim's Corvette, Larry heard his father tell the driver, "You can shut off the siren, the damage has already been done."

Larry never wanted to dive that morning, and if he hadn't, he thought, he wouldn't be a paraplegic today. There were plenty of if's to torment him and his family. If the hotel resort had placed "no trespassing" signs on the wall; if his father hadn't insisted on Larry coming with the family to Florida; if Tim hadn't pressured Larry to accompany him on a shark hunting trip that morning and the boat, loaded with two harpoon guns, hadn't been anchored off shore but tied to an accessible dock; if Larry had instead gone shopping with the young woman he met the night before as he wanted to; if he had trusted his own instinct to jump instead of dive. But if's were only illusions of control Larry and his family would imagine to convince themselves that they weren't powerless and subject to such tragedies.

The moment Larry dove into the ocean of an unimaginable future, his body—big and burly, veteran of fistfights, theft, carousing with musicians, guzzling bottles of beer, insensitive and out of touch with his feelings—was suddenly transformed into the body of a child. He was helpless, dependent, and angry.

In an instant, every value Larry held about the trustworthiness of life and other people was turned on end. He became aware of how vulnerable he was and how much he had really depended upon mercy or just plain good luck. For an adolescent to discover his vulnerability so completely was indeed terrifying. Tragedy showed Larry a truth greater than any he had ever known or ever wanted to know.

If God enters a man through his wounds, then the God that entered Larry was immense because his wound was so great. In less than three minutes, he surrendered life as he had known it and now had to travel what poet Robert Bly called in his book *Iron John* "the road of ashes, descent, and grief."

After more than a year of physical therapy at a rehabilitation center and hospital, Larry was able to go home. He started drinking heavily, but unlike the days when he guzzled cans of malt liquor with other boys along the Mississippi River under the City Bridge, he now depended on friends to lift the beer can to his mouth or steady the straw from which he sipped while in his wheel chair. He got drunk more often; his depression increased. Though his near-death vision convinced him of the existence of a Transcendent Being or Power, his experience of paralysis was so overwhelming it left no room for spiritual considerations.

Life for Larry was merciless and horrifying, and he attempted suicide. With limited use of his hands at that time and clever manipulation, he was able to remove sleeping pills from his mouth each night after the nurse gave them to him. He stored them in a nightstand drawer. One night, when he thought he had enough pills saved up, he took them all. In the worst of times, he had lost hold of the memory of his spiritual experience.

Obviously, Larry's revelation of a merciful God while he floated in the ocean did not bring him into a life of religious conviction and serenity. He was saved from drowning, but not from the difficulties and troubles ahead. His spiritual moment, though dramatic, did not remove the obstacles. Instead it provided him with a beacon, a memory, a thread that would return him to his soul. Sacred moments do not end a man's journey, but rather begin new journeys on roads that aren't often considered or imagined. Larry's prayer and revelation did not blissfully lift him into the celestial realms of acceptance, but rather allowed him to descend into a greater consciousness of the human condition where safety and indestructibility were only illusions. Larry's unwelcome task now was to recognize and accept completely the vulnerability of human life. He now knew his own existence could be blown away like a leaf by the wind. The sky truly could fall at any moment. How could he go on trusting in life and relationships? How could he find acceptance when his situation defied it? This was the task that pressed him for resolution. Most people around him hadn't an inkling of the depth of his spiritual crisis.

Looking back more than thirty years later, Larry believed that God and "the holiest and highest of all prayers" had saved him, though he admitted it was certainly possible to have been saved without saying the prayer. For him, the point wasn't whether he owed his life to God, Tim, or both, but that his experience of "the voice" revealed a depth of existence that profoundly affected him for the rest of his life. Larry perceived the Holy within the biological. He knew that even breathing itself, opening the mouth, inhaling air, letting the lungs and chest fill with life, and exhaling was surely a precious gift.

"After the diving accident," Larry reported, "I was always on this search to find the meaning of God. I always had this belief in God after that. There was something a lot more than just me, just us."

Though he had begun his search, he did not at first turn to the traditional resources of his religion and culture. For Larry, Judaism offered no easy answers, even if they were centuries old, that allowed him to escape the brutal realities of his paralysis. But he had begun a spiritual quest. Undaunted by the sheer physical difficulties of maneuvering himself in his wheelchair, his quest took him all over the world to study: in Greece, he visited and read about the ancient sites of the Minoans; in South America he studied the Inca, and in Mexico, the Mayan culture.

In 1961, Larry drove his van to Guadalajara, Mexico, where he lived in a boarding home. In a few years he learned to speak Spanish fluently. He eventually married in Mexico and raised two children. During the Vietnam war he managed a housing complex of ten bungalows called the Hacienda Las Fuentes—The Fountains—a resort for disabled Vietnam Vets which featured a wheelchair-accessible swimming pool. Larry trained his Mexican staff to work with war veterans with spinal cord injuries who traveled from the States to stay at his center. His house was dramatized in the movie *Born on the Fourth of July* as a resort which included procuring Mexican prostitutes for the vets as part of the services it offered, but Larry said the house actually was "a gentle place."

Twenty years later, after a divorce and a life of Odyssean travels, Larry was encouraged by a friend to consider his own religious roots in Israel as a spiritual source.

When he arrived in Jerusalem in 1980, he felt a profound sense of belonging. "I was home, there was no need to go searching for other religions and cultures," Larry said. "I was with my people. It was obvious to me that the world began here. I was in the middle of three major civilizations symbolized by Bethlehem, the birthplace of Christ for Christianity, the holy dome or rock, one of the two holiest places in the world for Moslems, and Israel—the Jews' Promised Land.

One afternoon Larry was sitting in his wheelchair at a small table in a plaza less than a hundred yards from Jerusalem's sacred Wailing Wall, drinking coffee and watching people. A Rabbi, not much older than Larry, approached and invited him to visit the Wailing Wall. This Rabbi's role was to look for men who appeared to be in spiritual need.

At the Wailing Wall, the Rabbi left Larry with another, older orthodox man with a long white beard and a paternal demeanor. He initiated Larry to the ancient, sacred ritual of putting on the Tefillin, wrapping around the left arm strips of leather with a small box attached to one. Larry asked about the box and was stunned to learn what was inside. Sealed inside the box was the Shema prayer, the very words he uttered before nearly drowning over twenty years ago!

Larry confided his near-death experience and the saying of the holy prayer to the older Rabbi. He had never yet spoken about it to anyone. When he revealed his secret to the Rabbi, who called his experience a true vision, the conflict he had with religion was suddenly resolved. Once the secret was told, it no longer belonged to him alone. The unspeakable had acquired a voice, and the words he spoke to another human being inevitably gave meaning his secrecy could not achieve.

Larry's chance meeting with the Rabbi began an intensive six-month study of the Torah. He had never attended synagogue regularly before, but now he became formally involved in religion and studied Judaism. He read the Torah each day.

Larry's decision to practice Judaism became an affirmation of his sacred moment. Putting on the Tefillin symbolically illustrated for him the origin of the word "religion," to bind or link the individual to God. His commitment was further deepened by his new work in Israel as a counselor for six adolescent Jewish boys from Australia, England, South Africa, and the United States.

Long after he left Israel, Larry's interest in music blossomed. By 1985, he was writing songs and performing as a singer with nationally renowned musicians. He sang throughout the country about disability.

One day, after performing for an audience of more than ten thousand people, Larry was hospitalized in New Jersey across from Giants Stadium with endotracheal tubes down his throat. While hooked to a respirator, he refused to allow the doctors to perform a tracheotomy on him. Not to be able to speak or sing, on top of his paralysis, was unthinkable. Although he recovered, two years later he was again hospitalized for pneumonia and again refused a tracheotomy. "I lay in intensive care for two months watching people die. I realized I was dying. A couple of times I felt myself literally lifting off the bed to float away. It happened twice. I realized at that moment I had a choice whether I wanted to die. All I had to do was let go. But something in me, I don't know what it was, maybe you could call it the will to live—doctors call it plain stubbornness—but I dug in and wouldn't let go. Then this upward lifting from the bed stopped. It was another affirmation that God can make Himself apparent in all kinds of ways."

Four months later Larry was discharged from the hospital, only to return finally for a tracheotomy because of another bout with pneumonia.

"Quests for living a meaningful life are common," Larry wrote in what will be his autobiography, *The Sound of My Wheels.* "But a quest to make sense of one's life in the face of adversity and injury are usually quiet struggles for dignity."

"God has shown me in a lot of ways why I'm around." Larry said. With a humility that characterized all the men interviewed in this book, he said, "I don't know anything about those terms: spirituality and awakening—that stuff. All I know is that these things happened."

He discussed how important it is for a man, in his struggle for dignity, not to hide his suffering but to draw sustenance and connection to others from it.

"Suffering makes a man a more sensitive person. One has to suffer a little bit to become more sensitive to what's going on. The guy who hasn't had any tragedies, no sickness, no suffering, I can tell. A traumatic injury like mine—and living with it—makes me a more sensitive person. Everyone I know who is disabled, suffering, or dying, is more aware of what they make of their time."

Connection to others through suffering reveals how relationships play an important role in men's spirituality. How their relationships are conducted on earth inevitably reflect on their relationship to God. If a man can't open himself to the forgiveness, compassion, and love from his wife, parents, family, and friends, he can't open himself to God for the same things. "I think men have a harder time focusing on spirituality because God and man is a relationship," Larry said. "A man has to open his heart and mind up."

After thirty-two years in a wheelchair, Larry has seen many acquaintances who were paralyzed like him die, and the imminence of his own death continues to motivate him to do charitable work. He continues to direct a state Home Care Advocacy Program to help get handicapped people out of institutions so they can lead independent lives at home. He has also participated in a university medical school's human sexuality program to sensitize students to sexual issues that affect disabled people.

"In the Jewish faith, doing a good deed, or mitzva, is a holy thing," Larry said. "The highest mitzva is giving to a charity anonymously. The more you help others the more you help yourself. Charity is the highest thing you can do. Service is the highest. Just to give money to a worthwhile charity that helps other people is a very high thing to do.

"I learned that I have to help others. I have to connect with my Judaism. I try to obey the rules, and lean towards orthodoxy by following Torah law, which includes a kosher diet, observing all the religious holidays, and praying every day. It's not enough to say you believe in God, but you've got to literally wrap yourself in God."

Today Larry is nearly fifty years old, and he reads each morning and evening from the sacred Siddur, a book of prayers. He keeps a small box called a mezuza posted near the door of his house. The box contains the Shema prayer—the prayer Larry said when he was about to drown, the prayer other Jews have prayed for centuries and will pray for centuries after him, the prayer of the Eternal who Larry experienced when he was just a boy floating in the ocean.

CHAPTER 4

The Orange Hologram

*The mystics insist that small things, far from
being inconsequential, are of special significance.*
                                                    —Patrick Grant

Jonathan got out of bed that Sunday morning a little after eight. Normally during the week, his alarm
buzzed at six, and he quickly got up, dressed,
washed, had a bowl of cereal, and left to catch the
bus to the State Department where he worked as an
information and speech writer.

That Sunday was Earth Day. After Jonathan put
on his trousers and walked barefoot into the living
room, he turned on the television to watch his
favorite Sunday morning news program. All week,
radio and television aired specials on pollution, the
depletion of the ozone layer, the accumulation of
nuclear waste, and other issues. The stable, square

49

picture on his thirteen-inch television allowed Jonathan, legally blind, to view the show easily from a distance of four to five feet while sitting on the floor. Forty-eight years old and blind for the last ten years with retinitis pigmentosa, a genetic disorder causing an inflammation of the retina, he described television as his "best source of reality." Reading was especially difficult because the constant movement of the eyes caused him to miss letters and parts of words. Trouble with his vision began in his adolescence with night blindness. Later his eyesight deteriorated into tunnel vision. He also had a hearing impairment related to his blindness called Usher's Syndrome, which required a hearing aid. Jonathan was a thin man, with light brown hair and a receding hair line. He leaned forward slightly when he walked.

After selecting a channel, he walked into his long, narrow kitchen to prepare breakfast. He took a bowl from the basin where the dishes were left the night before to dry, a box of cereal from the cupboard, and an orange from the refrigerator. The counter was cluttered, and he cleared a place to cut the orange in front of the kitchen window.

"I took a knife from the drawer," Jonathan reported, "and gripped the orange firmly between my thumb and two fingers. Because my blindness made me focus on things intensely, I normally scanned things bit by bit in order to see the general in a lot of particulars, but the orange nearly filled my field of vision."

His recall of details was vivid and exact. "Usually I lined up the orange carefully and cut right down from stem to blossom end, a nice cut right through the central axis of the orange, and then I got neat little quarters. That morning, I didn't cut it exactly, but slightly at an angle off the axis."

Precisely at the moment it fell open in a shaft of late morning light, Jonathan was unexpectedly overwhelmed by the extraordinary appearance of the orange. "It astounded me because it was so beautiful and illuminating," he said. "I had never seen an orange—anything—in that way. It was incredibly moist, glistening, very bright and intense in the sunlight. I was startled. It seemed to radiate light, not just catch it. It was actually its own source of illumination, spilling light out while the juice and smell pervaded the air. It created a strange kaleidoscopic effect. The surface was marbleized, roseate, like an opal, swirly, milky, and iridescent." It reminded him of a picture of the earth he had seen once. The swirly pattern of the orange's white fibers streaked the darker orange surface in the same way white vapor might streak the planet Earth as seen from outer space.

Jonathan experienced a profound moment of life's unity. "It was like the whole beauty of the Earth was spilling out of the orange, all of its freshness, its liquid, the smell. Everything was suddenly disclosed to me in the simple reality of that orange. I thought I had cut into a secret of the Earth, and the Earth had suddenly yielded up all its richness and abundance. All the rains that fell on the Earth, all the soil that nurtured the trees, the cycle of the seasons, the sun—everything was in that beautiful orange. I verbalize this now, but it was not the same as experiencing that moment. It wasn't a thought process, but a spontaneous experience which revealed itself to me all at once, like an Epiphany."

Jonathan's sudden illumination of the orange as a hologram reminds one of Julian of Norwich, a fourteenth century mystic, who also was awed by a revelation when she held "something small, no bigger than a hazelnut, lying in the palm of (her) hand." Both of their visions of the infinite in something as small as an orange or hazelnut reveal how, as in every hologram, the part manifests the whole.

Jonathan not only saw and smelled the orange but the sun, the earth, rain, soil, the seasons, and the life-force from which one thing is all things. The orange was simultaneously itself and more. In his vision, "everything was suddenly disclosed." The orange was no longer limited to a definition of its color, shape, and smell, but included and represented the universe. He saw the infinite in the smallest detail, as described by the poet William Blake:

To see a world in a Grain of Sand
And Heaven in a Wild Flower
Hold Infinity in the palm of your hand
And Eternity in an hour.

For Jonathan, the ordinary boundaries of time and space collapsed and were suspended. He could not pinpoint the exact moment his perception expanded into an extraordinary vision that could not be confused with the everyday. He experienced the profound "bliss" that author Nona Coxhead in *The Relevance of Bliss* identified as the key affective element of mystical experiences.

His sacred moment was typically brief, yet immeasurable in some way. "I don't think it lasted too long. It's hard to say, but I felt very moved, excited. I knew what Earth Day was about and I thought of the Earth as this beautiful opalescent orange marble against the darkness of space. The Earth was a living glistening jewel, so precious and rare in all that emptiness. I connected the jewel-like surface of the orange to the jewel of the Earth, radiant in the dull, dark universe. I felt in awe of the orange, of the Earth, of the precariousness and beauty of it all."

After his bliss waned, he returned to a more normal state of mind in the kitchen. Jonathan did eat the orange, but not in any way that he would describe as ordinary. His consumption of it was as

reverential as taking communion, and he understood for the first time the ritual of saying grace
before meals.

"I understood why people prayed at mealtime. It
was more than giving thanks for the bounty of the
Earth. Prayer was a gesture of humility, an acknowl-
edgment that we destroy in knowing, that we were
one with the vanquished. There was only one way of
knowing that did not destroy, and that was love.
Despite my revelation, I ate the orange, its beauty
and life. There was something terrible about eating
the orange, and prayer mitigated that."

After eating breakfast, he watched his news program, did housecleaning, paid bills, and went out to
visit a friend. Though his day was ordinary on one
level, on another his inner life had been powerfully
enriched.

Jonathan described the experience as a center
around which his daily activities revolved. The
moment in the kitchen with the orange "became a
hub around which other thoughts and feelings col-
lected. I carried it with me, nourished by that
moment throughout that day and for weeks afterwards," he said.

Jonathan would often mentally picture the orange
while sitting at his desk or walking down the street.
"Of course, it caused me to think practically about
environmental issues, but other emotions and
thoughts occurred that I couldn't explain," he said,

stressing how his revelation included but transcended political concerns about the environment.

"It wasn't just a practical, moral lesson about the environment." It revealed larger issues, like the mystery of creation itself and the preciousness of life. Concern for the environment was just a part of a very important center that I kept coming back to, kept remembering. Eventually, I wrote about it because writing for me was the expression of the spiritual and how that moment connected with the rest of my life."

He didn't want to speculate about the origin of his vision. "You could explain the experience by referring to all the hoopla of Earth Day," he said. "Or maybe I was especially hungry that morning, and the orange just happened to be situated perfectly in the shaft of sunlight, and I cut it just right. There were all kinds of material circumstances that might explain the sensory impact of the orange falling open, but it was more than that. Nothing could adequately explain how or why it happened. There's a mystery there."

When asked if he identified the "mystery" as a direct revelation of God, Jonathan said, "I'm an agnostic, and I wouldn't generalize like that, though I felt a sense of wonder, beauty, and power of life. I didn't extrapolate to some sense of Deity. I didn't go beyond the experience and say there must be some divine order or principle in the universe."

Though many people would attribute the transcendence and illumination he felt to God, Jonathan attributed it to the essence of the human spirit. "I'm more inclined to say that the human spirit is tremendous," he stated. "My experience gave me a sense of connection to life that I didn't have. My blindness tended to be isolating, and it reinforced a kind of brooding in me, but that moment brought me ecstasy and freedom. It mattered that people had a sense of the beauty or the wonder of creation because it was a part of humanity, but beyond that I didn't speculate. When I heard stories of courage and self-sacrifice, I didn't think, 'wasn't God wonderful!' I thought 'aren't human beings magnificent, full of god-like potential and qualities!'"

His comments reveal spiritual depth. His agnosticism shouldn't be seen as resistance against God but support for humanity and its fathomless potential for love and relatedness.

"I accepted things the way they were because they made life bearable. More than bearable! They made life glorious! Now, there's a place in myself where I can go to or tap and feel that sense of awe and beauty. I believe it's there—that place inside," a place for Jonathan which is as sacred as any church or temple.

But Jonathan couldn't return to that place at will. He wasn't Ali Baba of the Arabian Nights, able to command a door to open to the riches of his soul by saying, "Open Sesame!" When Jesus advises: "Knock, and it shall be opened unto you," one shouldn't interpret the knock as a inadvertent tap that opens the door to heaven. Jesus said also, "Ask, and it shall be given you; seek, and you shall find." It is not by magic that Jonathan or any man is gifted with a sacred moment. One must ask and seek. Though an element of chance characterizes these revelations, grace and receptivity, more than magic or luck, allow the moment to happen. Jonathan stresses the importance of seeking and being receptive to the sacred moment.

"There's a cultivation of a state of being that's necessary," he asserted. Awareness of the sacred and life's unity had to be nurtured or it would be lost. A man must attend to his soul as well as to his body.

Another experience illustrated the importance Jonathan placed on the cultivation of the spiritual and how the efficacy of a spiritual experience can be lost if the moment is not completely attended to.

Early one evening in June, months after his Earth Day experience, Jonathan was preparing to give a massage at an AIDS clinic to a Baptist man who had tested HIV positive. (Jonathan did volunteer service for the agency after completing a twenty-hour training course in giving massages.)

"This man I'll call Robert was very religious," Jonathan related. "He turned a lot of his life over to

God. I liked him, respected him, and had given him weekly massages over the last year. Generally he was quite restrained and nonverbal, and he didn't talk much about his personal life. He was always poised and calm, but when he talked about his relationship to God, he became excited, eloquent, like a poet. His language was beautiful, very coherent, and fluent."

That evening, Jonathan laid a sheet over the massage table and left the room as Robert undressed to lay on the table for his massage. When Jonathan returned to the room, he poured lotion into his hands, rubbing them together in order to warm the lotion. He began the massage with a movement called effleurage, a long sweeping stroke that spread the lotion up the back from the base of the spine, out over the shoulder blades, and down the sides in the configuration of a butterfly.

For the first half hour, the two men discussed various subjects, especially the issue of adoption of black children. That evening, Robert was especially talkative because the subject concerned his own work with churches and placing black children in black homes. As Robert talked, lying face down on the table, Jonathan continued massaging him.

When Robert turned over, Jonathan moved to the end of the table and crouched to get a better angle to massage Robert's leathery feet. Jonathan kneaded the inside sole of one foot with his thumbs, beginning at the heel, up to the big toe and down again. He massaged from the inside of the foot across the center to the outside. Just as he began to repeat the process, he suddenly found himself emotionally swept up in a second illumination.

"I was still crouched down when suddenly it hit me that this man, Robert, was a child of God. I knew it sounded weird. Normally I would never say anything like that about somebody. Sometimes I felt very reverential about doing massages on people and thought different things, but at that moment all my thoughts left. I was overwhelmed, and felt that I was touching the body of a holy person. I was overcome by the holiness of his body, of the body itself, of his being, the holiness of my connection to him. I truly believed that he was a child of God. I was close to crying."

As tears moistened his eyes, Jonathan finished the foot and rose to stand when it occurred to him that "if he was a child of God, then I was a child of God." That conclusion, the sudden perception of his own divinity, startled and panicked Jonathan. He accepted Robert's holiness, the holiness of the human body in general, but he could not accept his own. The revelation cut across the grain of his own agnosticism. To be a child of God would mean that Jonathan believed in God.

While most sacred moments deepen, affirm, and comfort a man in his belief, Jonathan's confronted and challenged him. He was on the verge of a dramatic conversion. Most of the transformations men underwent took place over a long period of time. Instead, Jonathan was ready to burst immediately into a new, but threatening light. "I got nervous. I turned the revelation into a joke, smirked, and said to myself, 'this is preposterous.' Suddenly the spell was broken and the holy feeling was diffused and scattered." Jonathan's reverie vanished as suddenly as it had appeared.

"I had an intuition about a truth, not only about Robert, but about myself, about anybody. It was like a spark that wanted to jump from him to me, but I wouldn't let it."

In Psalms 46:10, we are advised to "be still, and know." But Jonathan could not be still and maintain an inner composure to receive any further revelation while massaging Robert. "I often thought of myself as a mere speck floating around in the universe, but that vision was really telling me something else."

Unlike his vision of the orange that resonated like a chord of music for weeks, the sacred moment he had while massaging Robert's feet ended abruptly, as if his own lack of reception served as a brake to any further revelation.

As a child, Jonathan had felt close to God. "I remember walking home from school having long conversations with God, and I can remember seeing the face of God in the moon, encircled by clouds. I had a visceral sense of the reality of God. I saw it in my daughter when she was growing up. She also carried God around with her. The poet Wordsworth wasn't lying about children 'trailing clouds of immortality.' That's the way you came into the world. My daughter often talked to God. She'd stand in the driveway, look up to the sky, and just talk to him. She'd throw theological questions at me and be generally dissatisfied with my answers. Somehow I lost touch with that childlike connection. I think those experiences with the orange and Robert are traces, vestiges, echoes of the unity I had as a child, long ago."

Jonathan remembered as a boy listening to his grandfather, an agnostic, talk at home about the "hypocrisy of Christians." His grandfather often referred to Christ driving out the money changers from the temple as God's admonitions against the wealthy. "He thought Christians were too concerned about money and material things," Jonathan said.

His parents didn't attend church services, though his mother encouraged him and his brother to attend. Jonathan belonged to a Protestant church until he was a young adult. His very personal faith confronted by a highly doctrinal church and family indifference produced a volatile mix in him.

When he was twenty-two, he recalled going to his

pastor to tell him, "I don't believe in the doctrines of the church anymore, nor in exclusive salvation through Jesus. That wasn't the only way people could be saved. I told him I wasn't going to church anymore.

"For nineteen years I didn't go to church. Then my daughter, thirteen years old, insisted on being baptized. I finally said okay, and we started going to a neighborhood parochial church and Sunday school. Just before her confirmation she pulled out and I left the church again. While she was going to church, it meant something to me, but after I left I never regretted it."

Though Jonathan today has no religious affiliation, he has begun to reevaluate spirituality and what it means to him. "I've never been comfortable with the word 'spiritual' and don't often apply it to myself. When other people use the word, I think they may be too pretentious. However, some strange things have been happening. Last month I read an essay about the spirituality of the writing process, and I was so excited, so hungry for everything the author was saying, I kept reading even though reading was especially hard for me. I thought the author, who was explaining writing in terms of a spiritual process, was speaking directly to me. I would never have paid any heed to it before, but I said to myself I would take a writing class from the author, and I did. My own writing lately is moving in another direction, a spiritual direction, and then you called out of the blue."

Jonathan showed the same humility and openness as all the other men I interviewed. Service to others at the AIDS center was important to him. His heartfelt belief in the beauty and preciousness of the Human Spirit and the Earth reflected his sense of reverence. Despite his self-criticism, Jonathan is receptive to those rare moments when a man is suddenly given a deeper vision of life. Author Evelyn Underhill describes men like Jonathan as becoming "aware of an unchanging love and beauty which really transformed their lives...in which the elements of common life are given new colour and worth." Jonathan has shown us the "common life" of a simple orange, its profound "colour and worth."

CHAPTER 5

Both Father and Son

Forgive us...as we forgive.

— Matt. 6:12

Duane grew up as a Methodist in a small, midwest-
ern town where his father owned a monument business, lettering and engraving tombstones. Wanting
no part of the business, Duane left home after high
school for Grinnell College. A bright and indus-
trious student, he graduated Phi Beta Kappa and
went on as a Rhodes scholar to study at Oxford
where he graduated with a first class degree in phi-
losophy, politics, and economics. When he returned
to the United States, he attended the University of
Chicago law school and again he graduated with
honors.

As one might expect of a young man with academic credentials such as Duane's, once out of school,

his career immediately rocketed. Only twenty-eight years old, he was soon orbiting among power brokers, bankers, and litigation lawyers on Wall Street in New York. His first job put him among the "stars" in the prestigious law firm of Cravath, Swaine and Moore. With an office on the fifty-seventh floor of the Chase Manhattan Building, Duane had an aerial view of the New York Harbor and Statue of Liberty. His work involved him in corporate ligation, drafting pleadings, interrogatories, document demands, briefs, conducting the first deposition and trial, and interviewing and preparing witnesses. He worked on government contract issues and distinguished cases—he wrote the brief for the House of Representatives and U.S. Supreme Court in the Adam Clayton Powell case.

Duane lived in Brooklyn Heights across the Brooklyn Bridge from Wall Street. Happily married with two sons, his life looked more than promising. "There was no room in my life for God and a spiritual life," he said. At first, the intense life as a young Wall Street lawyer thrilled Duane, but within four short years, he became disenchanted with the fast pace of metropolitan life in New York. The stress, traffic, crowds of people jostling each other on the street, and noise made him yearn for the Midwest. He and his family soon decided to leave New York and start a new life in Minneapolis.

Duane again found work in litigation for one of

the most prestigious and wealthiest firms in the city, which now employs 240 lawyers on seven floors in a downtown building. By 1981, in his early forties, Duane had by all outward signs matured into a successful lawyer. However, all the while, his sense of purpose and meaning in life was deteriorating. He described his state as "an inner emptiness and lack of purpose."

In the years since leaving his childhood home, Duane never considered going to church. "I thought religion was an antiquated superstition of no use to intelligent educated people." But his "emptiness" and desperation now motivated him to reconsider religion, and "after twenty-five years of neglect" Duane began attending a local Presbyterian church. The church offered intelligent sermons and high quality music, and it allowed him as much or as little participation as he wished. It was a safe and comforting place for a skeptical man in spiritual need like Duane. Soon after, crises had developed both in Duane's family and in his professional life.

Duane's oldest son had begun experimenting with drugs at school and with friends on weekends. Once a good student and athlete, his grades dropped and his interest in sports waned. As a junior in high school, he became truant, skipping classes and heavily abusing alcohol and drugs. At home, he was incorrigible, sarcastic, and hostile to his parents. No matter how many curfews Duane set, his son ignored them, staying out late every weekend. Some nights he never came home and returning early in the morning offered no explanation of where he spent the night.

One evening in early May 1984, Duane and his wife, having already once committed their son to chemical dependency treatment, finally agreed that he must leave the house. At first, Duane resisted the idea of evicting his son. "I understood her conclusion, but I could not carry it out," he remembered. But that night, he agreed that decisive and responsible action had to be taken immediately.

He called his son down from upstairs. The two sat in the living room, and Duane told him that his behavior could no longer be tolerated. "For the protection of the rest of the family, we couldn't live with him anymore," Duane explained. His son didn't argue with his dad and stared mindlessly across the room. "Be out of here in an hour," Duane ordered.

His son went back upstairs to his room, packed a few things, called a friend for a ride and left the house without a word to either of his parents. Before he left, Duane gave him $150.00, which angered his wife, who thought the money would only be spent on drugs.

"'Tough love' is too easy a phrase," Duane says now, yet there was no other choice at the time. During the next few months, he had no idea of his son's whereabouts, only that "he was living a desolate life."

Though his son often agreed to join his parents for dinner, he rarely showed. At home, Duane and his wife would set a place for him at the dinner table only to put away the clean dishes later. Early one Monday morning in June, their son was arrested for burglarizing a nearby home. He was put in detox, five months away from his eighteenth birthday.

All the while his son was gone, the memory of the last days Duane had spent with his own father haunted him. His father had died from a heart attack in an emergency room soon after Duane had driven him to the hospital. The day before, the two of them had argued about Duane's relationship with another high school friend. They never had a chance to reconcile before he died. Now, Duane feared that something similarly tragic would happen to him or his own son, leaving the other forever in remorse.

Hoping to find some relief for his pain, Duane availed himself of the resources of his church and asked his minister to lunch. It was late June, a sunny and warm afternoon. The two men stopped at a local deli, bought sandwiches and a drink, and walked to a nearby plaza, a favorite spot for downtown workers to have lunch next to Orchestra Hall. A tubular fountain cascaded water into a series of falls that flowed into a reflecting pool. Many workers stretched out on the green grass to eat their lunch. Duane and the minister sat on stone bench-like cubes.

Hoping to ease Duane's grief over the plight of his son, the minister recounted the parable of the Prodigal Son, hoping it might give Duane a context in which to consider his problems.

As he sat listening to the minister, Duane was overcome with emotion. As a child, he had heard the parable many times, but never did it carry such an intense visceral meaning for him as it did that afternoon. Now he understood how the father in the parable must have suffered while his son "wasted his substance with riotous living." All the while the minister talked during their lunch hour, Duane was nearly in tears. "Though the father's anger and hurt doesn't appear in the parable," Duane said, remembering the minister's words, "the father must have felt anger and pain," as he did. Duane's revelation in the plaza was the first time he felt connected to fathers across the centuries who experienced similar pain for their sons. "Yet the father in the parable overcomes the pain," Duane said. "He demonstrates what love is about—selfless and focused on the son's welfare.

"Then and ever since, it is the most meaningful passage in scripture for me," Duane said. "The parable provided me with comfort and instruction on how I should react to my son. I could put myself into the role of the father and draw instruction on how I should behave, act and feel." But Duane's revelation that afternoon involved more than learning how to respond to his son.

Once he understood how a father in a centuries old parable could offer him guidance, Duane could begin to forgive his son. But equally important, he opened himself in the plaza to forgiveness for his losses. Now able to give forgiveness, he could receive it as well.

The minister leaned across to Duane and asked him to see himself not just as the father in the parable, but also as the son. At that moment, tears again filled his eyes as he felt for the first time since he could remember the love of God welcoming him home. Now, he was the son, who "was dead, and is alive again...was lost, and is found."

Duane believed the parable held special meaning for men. "In the story, there's no mother present," he remembered. In fact, he thought the parable would lose force if it was the mother, not the father, welcoming the son. "Mothers are always supposed to love their children," he says today. "But Fathers in society are viewed as judgmental, and standoffish, not as welcoming and forgiving. The fact that the parent in the parable was a father makes it immensely more powerful for everyone, especially men."

A few years later, Duane's spiritual awakening to

love and forgiveness helped him to begin a second struggle. For a long time, he was troubled by the gulf between his professional and spiritual lives. He had come to believe that one's spiritual life *should* inform all aspects of a life, but his certainly didn't.

In 1986, Duane began to publicly explore these private issues. He gave a speech at the University of Iowa law school titled "The Pilgrimage of a Hired Gun," a pejorative term sometimes used to refer to litigation lawyers like himself. In his speech, he spoke of his "search for meaning and spiritual values." Still, at that time, his search had hardly begun.

Later that year, he was invited to Phoenix, Arizona, for a meeting with lawyers and religious leaders involved in the Sanctuary Movement, which provided housing and services for refugees from Central American countries who had come to the United States illegally, seeking political asylum. "But it was still a professional matter," Duane recalled. "It was the thing to do to become a better lawyer." He was soon involved in a lawsuit against the government, alleging that the Immigration and Naturalization Service was sending agents to infiltrate the Sanctuary Movement.

"As a lawyer, it was a great case," Duane remembered. But personally, his work in the Sanctuary Movement was simply building his professional skills. Though he was learning about immigration law, human rights committees, and pro bono asylum projects that trained lawyers to represent aliens fleeing prosecution, his motives were not entirely charitable. "It was mainly to help myself be a better lawyer," he said. "I was not motivated then to integrate my spiritual and professional life."

In January 1989, he volunteered to represent a Salvadoran man fleeing persecution in his country. Again, his motivation was primarily to build upon his knowledge of international law to become a more talented and knowledgeable lawyer. In this case, he needed to educate himself on the law of El Salvador. While preparing for his case, he learned about the life of Archbishop Oscar Romero, who was shot and murdered in March 1980 while saying mass in a small hospital chapel. In December, following his murder, four American church women were brutally raped, murdered, and thrown into a shallow grave. The news of the slayings appeared on front pages of newspapers throughout the world, while violence continued to be a daily threat for the Salvadoran people. Still, when Duane went to El Salvador in April 1989, he was essentially there to investigate for his current case and acquire more information. In essence, "to do a better job as a lawyer," he said. The very day he and fifteen others from the Sanctuary Movement arrived, the country's attorney general was killed by a car bomb.

The first site Duane's group visited was the metropolitan cathedral in the city of San Salvador. The cathedral is situated in the center of the city and opens onto a plaza. It was in that plaza, years earlier, that twenty-six people died when soldiers, positioned on top of the National Assembly Building across the street, opened fire on a crowd of thirty thousand attending Archbishop Romero's funeral.

Roads circle around the cathedral and the din of traffic, unmuffled trucks and cars, echoed inside. For Duane, the cathedral was a great surprise. It was nothing like the one in his city with beautiful granite, well-paved stone stairs, and a copper dome. Standing on cracked steps, he saw steel reinforcing rods protruding like spikes on the outside of the church, which was blackened with soot from car exhaust. Long ago, Romero had halted construction of the cathedral because of the poverty of the Salvadorans. He could not allow the house of God to be built when so many of his people were impoverished or homeless.

Inside, the cathedral was no better. "It was not a beautiful place," Duane said. Instead of polished oak pews, there were only crude uncomfortable wooden benches. Paint peeled off the cracked plastered walls. He remembered seeing linoleum, not marble, on the floors. The concrete walls were ugly and gray, and he remembered nothing remarkable about the altar. In the right transept of the cathedral was Romero's tomb with flowers and handwritten prayers for Romero left on it. Duane suddenly felt overwhelmed and nearly broke out crying.

"I stood by the tomb for a long time," he said. He spoke to no one in his group. Other Salvadorans came and went, all of them of course speaking Spanish. Duane didn't know Spanish, and even if he had, "I didn't want to talk to anyone," he said. While standing near the tomb in silence, he watched the Comadres women pass near him as they prayed at the tomb. The women, dressed in black dresses with hoods, represented a committee of mothers of people who had disappeared or were assassinated. Already, some of the mothers were held in detention by authorities investigating the killing of the attorney general.

In the cathedral, Duane remained silent, letting himself be swept into a newfound compassion for others. A phrase kept running through his mind: "My body broken for you. My body broken for you." He assumed the words were Christ's, spoken at the Last Supper and repeated in the sacrament of Communion in Christian Churches everywhere. Only now, for Duane, they described Romero as Christ-like. He felt that he was truly in the presence of God, in a holy place, at the tomb of a saint.

By the time he walked back down the cathedral steps, Duane had been transformed. He now felt that he had come to El Salvador not to be a better lawyer but to become a more loving and compassionate man. Outside, standing in the plaza, he was visibly shaken by the memory of the twenty-six people killed there. He was no longer the man who only thirty minutes earlier entered the church. Though it would take him years to realize what would come of his brief moment in the cathedral, Duane knew a dramatic change had taken place deep in his heart and soul.

Deeply reflective and still silent, Duane boarded the van with the others as they drove to the Comadres' headquarters, not far from the cathedral. There, Duane met one of the women who had been arrested and illegally detained earlier that day. As she spoke, Duane noticed a bust of Robert Kennedy behind her which commemorated a human rights award the Comadres had been given. They were not allowed a visa to come to America to receive the award, however, because the American government considered the women subversives.

Afterwards, Duane's group drove several miles away to the hospital chapel where Romero was killed, then to a second chapel on the campus of the University of Central America. In contrast to the cathedral, the University chapel was located on a hill outside the city. Trees, a beautiful green lawn and shrubbery surrounded the chapel. Duane noticed linen on the altar, candles, polished pews, plastered and painted walls, and curtains over windows. Murals were on the walls, along with spare and elegant drawings of tortured people and a bust of Romero. "With these people it is easy to be a good pastor," an inscription from Romero read. On the side, the walls were opened and screened. A gentle breeze blew in as Duane and his group listened and spoke with John Sobrino, a learned Jesuit liberation theologian.

Seven months after Duane returned home, six Jesuit priests, their housekeeper, and her daughter were murdered on the grounds of the University of Central America near the chapel where Duane had met Sobrino. The national guard came around midnight and ordered them outside to lie down on the ground. Each one was shot. At the time, Sobrino was away lecturing in Thailand. Duane was stunned when he heard the news and helped organize a noon vigil in downtown Minneapolis in honor of the people killed.

Today, Duane believes that his short while in the cathedral, along with his visit to the chapels, were sacred moments that clearly marked a deep change in his life. His religion helps him make sense of his experience in El Salvador, which translates to mean "The Savior."

"Romero spoke against repression, for love and reconciliation, like Christ," Duane said. "People in his country were subject to 'unjust structures' and the military." Now Duane was ready to join Christ and Romero to celebrate the love of the Christian gospel and speak out against the forces of injustice. He had found new joy and meaning in his work.

As a result, his work for the Sanctuary Movement, which was once simply professional, now was a way for him "to be connected to Romero, El Salvadorans, and give help to others who cross my path," Duane says. "Direct human assistance connects my spiritual life to my work life. I now experience joy in my work."

Duane reflected on the difference in his life now and the days in 1981 when he first returned to church. "As I see it, my twenty-five years of a spiritual wasteland from college to 1981 are very important to me. It strangely prepared me for my life now and contributes to my current spirituality." His wasteland or desert created a thirst in him for a meaningful life; it also gave him skills that he used later as a lawyer to help the suffering. "That period of no-life has made the quest for a spiritual life much more enriching," he said.

His two revelations, one with his minister in Minneapolis and the other in the San Salvador Cathedral, largely shaped the years that followed. Yet, For Duane, what preceded and followed those sacred moments was as meaningful as the moments themselves. He believes now that a "preparation phase" had to take place to make him receptive to the sacred moment. Then later, years of reflection on the moments themselves was necessary to discern their meanings. "When the event happened," he said, "its significance came about as a result of praying, writing, talking, and reflecting. The emotional and spiritual meaning of the time in the plaza and inside the cathedral deepened in time."

Religion plays an important role in Duane's life. "In America, too many people think that spirituality is private and personal," Duane said. "But in the congregation of fellow believers, you can draw support and sustenance in ways you can't when making your way through life alone."

For him, even the architecture of his church contributes to heightening his sense of community. "It gives me the feeling that you are indeed a member of a congregation. Anywhere you sit, you see peoples' faces, not just the backs of their heads. The stained glass windows are really present in that sanctuary; they feel very near you, not off in the distance like in some churches."

Duane still relies on support from his church and ministers, as well as friends, to deepen his spirituality. He readily quotes scripture to explain his understanding of God. "We only see the back of God," he says, remembering a passage from the Old Testament. "Only occasionally do we get glimpses of God who loves us in ways beyond our understanding," he added, teary-eyed. "I thought I caught a glimpse of God through what I went through with my son."

Duane sympathizes with men who find it difficult to believe in God, let alone attend church. "I think in our culture men are socialized to believe that they can be and should be in control of their own lives," he said. "As a result, you become a god, if you will, and do not need any outside power. Men are encouraged not to show their emotion, their vulnerability, not to admit they need someone else, a knowledge or power greater than themselves. It is very difficult to admit to a spiritual life in our society for men. My mission now is to be a witness to God's love, and that can be done in different ways. To do that in the big law firms and corporate America is difficult. I can't say I always do, but I think as a result of my own experiences I try with others in different groups. I share my essays with others by witnessing, giving testimony not in a legal but spiritual sense. My essays or lectures are my way of finding out how God works in my life. We each have to find a way to witness that is consistent with our gifts and personalities."

For Duane, his sacred moments create a kind of nucleus around which the rest of his life and activities cluster. He tries to connect his spiritual life to the community through personal writing, journals, lecturing, and involving himself as a church member in a "spiritual growth committee." Its purpose is to help members of the church explore and deepen their spirituality and awareness of God.

"There are disciplines that can be used to grow spirituality," Duane said, emphasizing the need for spiritual work. "Deepening your spirituality is a task that must be attended to consciously. It is not something that just happens to you. Sacred moments don't always announce themselves as 'wake up, this is what it means to you.' You only find out about it through reflection."

Rather than keep his sacred moments secret, Duane seeks opportunities to share his spiritual life in appropriate settings. "In my church there are moments of sharing when one person is asked to speak briefly about some matter of faith during the service," he explained. "When you verbalize what it is, you are emboldened to do it outside the confines of the church. I think we all need to engage in more conversation with other people. I feel a sense of duty to speak about these issues. I see myself today as vastly different than I was in 1981. In a sense, I am born again, but not in an evangelical way."

Though he was born twice as William James describes his experience, his birth was not a conversion. Begun by a sacred moment, his birth was only a start. It has taken him years to mature, to understand how a moment while having lunch in a plaza and standing in a cathedral can require a lifetime of devotion, patience, and forgiveness.

"I love my son," he says. "I am very proud of him. He is married now, has children of his own, and we have a good relationship."

Today, while meeting his son at a restaurant for dinner, he might pause at the table before sitting down. The early evening light that enters through the window falls on the table linen. As he pulls the chair out, he may again realize that he is not only the prodigal son, but a loving and forgiving father.

CHAPTER 6

In Two Places at Once

*It is safe to say that a man who has never tried
to flee God has never experienced the God Who
is really God.*

— Paul Tillich

"Am I my brother's keeper?" Cain answered when asked where Abel was. It is an answer I might have given twenty years ago if I were asked about the plight of my own brother, Tom, years younger than me and the youngest of us eight siblings. However, this summer afternoon, while interviewing him on the front porch, I could now express my regrets and be a witness to his life.

Tom's story begins in 1966. He was fifteen, walking the streets of a Cleveland suburb during the Christmas holidays. The snow-covered roads glistened under the street lights. Before reaching Duds

& Suds Laundromat in a small shopping center, he had passed homes and storefronts decorated with colorful lights, Nativity scenes, and pictures of Santa Claus pasted to windows.

Inside the laundromat, Tom took a screwdriver from his back pocket to pry out the coin boxes on the washers and dryers. As he stuffed nearly twenty-five dollars worth of quarters into his pockets, Tom spotted a police car cruising into the parking lot. He quickly picked up a magazine from the counter, sat down, crossed his legs, and tried to look like a customer waiting for his laundry. After the police car drove past, Tom walked out the front door and across the lot. Before he could reach the street, the policeman drove up behind him.

While most other boys his age were attending church, visiting relatives, or wrapping presents at home, Tom sat in the front seat of the squad car confessing to the burglary. The normal life of an adolescent boy was already impossible for him. He was driven to the police station and later to a juvenile detention center.

Determined not to stay at the center, Tom staged a rebellion, insulting the guards, kicking doors, and throwing a bench against a window. He was finally handcuffed and transported, along with two prostitutes, to the county jail in Cleveland on Christmas Eve, two days before his sixteenth birthday. Though the only other adolescents at county jail were two juveniles awaiting trial for murder, Tom thought himself fortunate, because there he was allowed to smoke cigarettes whenever he wanted. He had been considered incorrigible the year before, and was often truant from school and fighting.

While in county jail for two months, Tom grew increasingly depressed and no longer cared what happened to him. He confessed to an additional twenty-eight robberies that other youths he knew had committed. At his trial he was sentenced to an indefinite stay at George Junior Republic in Grove City, Pennsylvania, a group home for incorrigible youths, the last stop before adult prison.

The judge allowed Tom one day of freedom at home before his sentence at the Pennsylvania center began. Late that night, the entire family urged him to go to bed, but Tom insisted on staying up. I had decided to sit up with him, watching television in the family room. Though worried about him, I felt relieved that at least he was spending the evening at home.

By midnight, I grew tired and went to bed upstairs, leaving Tom alone. Everyone else had already retired. Long after I was asleep, Tom went to the basement where he had hidden a stolen .22 caliber pistol in a corner under some boxes. He sat down in a chair and turned on the basement television set. In a short time, while a program aired, Tom casually stuck the gun in his mouth.

He suddenly thought about our parents, sleeping in the bedroom directly above him. He imagined the bullet projecting through the ceiling and striking either our father or mother. He didn't want that to happen and took the gun out of his mouth. He went back upstairs and left the house for a nearby woods with the pistol tucked in his pocket.

Outside, halfway up the street, was a field with bushes and small trees. Tom was crossing the field when a police car turned onto the street. Spotted by the officers, Tom threw the gun into the weeds. After questioning him, the police took him to the station where Tom managed to wrap the bullets in his pocket in tissue and flush them down the toilet to escape detection. Though the police had inadvertently saved his life, Tom's suicide attempt went undetected. He spent his one night of freedom sleeping with his head on the police sergeant's desk. The following morning I sat with him in the station before he was driven to Pennsylvania. Though he was fortunate to be alive, Tom would not have thought so.

Soon after, I returned for my last year of study at a boarding school in upstate New York where I was oblivious for years of Tom's crisis.

At the juvenile home, Tom was never alone. He was escorted by senior adolescent trustees to each of his classes and to his cottage after school. Hoping to avoid additional school hours, Tom agreed to barber training at the center to learn to cut and style hair in the afternoons.

He completed his training, as well as part of his tenth grade education, and was released in November 1967. To get licensed in Ohio, prior arrangements were made for Tom to attend barber college. He thought his decision to be a barber was based simply on the large tips, flexible hours, and independence he imagined for himself. Though life for Tom was now more hopeful, he had six days to pass at home before starting barber college.

With no one watching, telling him where to go and when to be there, he wondered if the idle time would lead him back into burglary, fist fights, and drinking. He was sixteen years old, and for the first time in nearly a year, no one stood guard over him. "I used to pray then and ask God to keep me out of trouble," Tom remembered. "I didn't have much faith that God would help because He wanted me to pay for my sins. I prayed because I grew up that way. I was told to ask for help, so I did. They were the toughest six days I ever lived." Tom played solitaire and read Alfred Hitchcock anthologies to pass the time at home.

Once in barber college, he felt relieved and more confident. His training at the juvenile center gave him an advantage over other students who hadn't any prior instruction. When business was slow, Tom was encouraged to take additional breaks so the others, less experienced, could get more time styling hair. During these breaks, he often walked to the delicatessen on Denison Avenue to buy cigarettes, pop, or gum. Sometimes he walked to the bank to buy and examine rolls of quarters and dimes for his coin collection.

One December morning, he put on the brown suede coat with a fur collar that one of our sisters had bought for him. Underneath it he wore his white barber smock buttoned over the shoulder. "It was cold outside, around ten in the morning, and snow covered the ground when I left for the delicatessen. It was fascinating to just walk down the street and have no one watching me. I could buy cigars or cigarettes without having to account to anyone how I got the money."

In the delicatessen, Tom noticed a well-dressed man at the counter. "He had a business suit on and looked like a model in a men's magazine. He was about thirty-five, tall, trim, and confident, like a banker." Standing behind him, Tom watched the man reach into his pockets for money as he asked for cigarettes. "I thought to myself 'someday I want to be like that man and wear a suit.' I could walk into a store in the middle of the day to buy cigarettes, smile, and nobody would tell me what to do. I'd have a nice car, too."

The man smiled and thanked the clerk as Tom watched him put the cigarettes in his suit coat and walk out. The man's poise and contentment intrigued Tom. "Most of all, I'd be happy and confident like I imagined him," Tom said. He bought a pack of Camels and left the store, feeling strangely excited.

"The sun had come out and was warm on my face," he remembered. "I hadn't walked even a half a block when a feeling suddenly came over me. I looked up to the sky and an intense, unexplainable feeling came over me. Something was taken or pulled out of my body. My skin tingled. I remember smiling, which was something I rarely did then. I had a sense that something supernatural was in charge.

"I could only explain that feeling by an analogy. It was as if I always had a glass rod stuck through my arm, sticking half in and half out, and at that moment on the street the glass was removed. I felt pressure in my body, but no pain. Something pulled the rod out nice and smoothly. It was like that," Tom reported. "Negativism from my feet to the top of my head was lifted out of me."

Tom's analogy might very well be archetypal, since it appears in Hans Christian Andersen's, *Snow Queen*. The tale—which Tom had never read—explains how people's perceptions get so skewed they become cynical and hopeless. In the *Snow Queen*, evil trolls drop their mirror from the sky and "the wind blew the pieces everywhere."

Glass chards and slivers lodged in people's bodies, in their eyes and hearts. Afterwards, "nothing looked right again." They quickly became negative and cynical. The only way they might find happiness again was to have the glass removed. Not until Kai in Andersen's story can remember how to spell the word "eternity" which he had forgotten and cry to wash the glass out of his eye does joy return. Tom, too, could not experience joy or have the "glass" removed from his body until he remembered eternity or "something supernatural" that he had lost.

"I felt peace and serenity," Tom said. "Nothing was going to happen to me. Something supernatural was in charge. I knew that I wasn't doomed. I looked down the street and all my worries, fears, and thoughts went away. I knew things would be better, forever, and I'd be okay. All I had to do was what I was doing. I didn't have to try any harder. To me, it was amazing! It felt good. I knew there was a caring, warm, and loving force or energy, but I didn't call it God or Higher Power at that time."

On the street, Tom felt joyful and confident. "In the future," he concluded, "I didn't always have to be who I was." When he returned to the barber college, he felt happy for the first time since he could remember.

Tom further explained his sacred moment. "I asked for help everyday when I walked to the store because I was afraid to go home after barber college. I didn't know what I was going to do and I didn't want any idle time. I think that's why that happened—because I asked for help."

The benefit was immediate. "After that day went by, I always thought there was a positive energy around me, but I had to think about the energy in order to feel it. It was all over me, inside me and surrounding me. A week later, I was still thinking about this positive energy and I didn't worry as much about getting into trouble. In chemistry, opposites like electrons and protons repel each other and won't collide because there's a force that holds them apart. The force I had was positive and repelled negative things, helping me as long as I thought good thoughts. It was kind of dumb because something that simple couldn't be that powerful. But it was! If I didn't think negatively about burglary and fighting, I'd be okay."

The spiritual moment that expanded Tom's consciousness immediately increased his self-control. No longer leashed to his impulses, he relaxed and assumed more responsibility from his "Force," a personal transcendent power that he appealed to for help. "I talked to it and knew what it was," Tom said. Still, he continued to pray and pay deference to his old God "just in case." Tom stayed away from fights and stealing and tried to picture himself as "a good guy." Though his transformation from juvenile delinquent to good guy wouldn't be easy, he now had a spiritual force to help and made quick progress.

Our entire family was happy and relieved with the new attitude Tom seemed to show. Within a year after his experience he was licensed as a barber, admitted to the union, employed full time, and enrolled in a course to earn his high school diploma. On weekends, he moonlighted as a house painter in a summer business that another brother and I had started.

Tom's success gave him self-confidence, but he began to take his good fortune for granted. "I was still thinking about my force, but not as much," he reported. "I was saving for a car, playing pool in bars, dating, studying for school. I had friends and obligations." Because he felt he didn't need help, he stopped asking for it. When he received his high school degree in 1970, his sacred moment outside the delicatessen was like the sun setting on the horizon, losing warmth and influence.

Years earlier, when Tom was fourteen, he was taking a bath one afternoon when he suddenly sloped down in the tub and went unconscious. When he was found, the water level was right below his chin. He had gone into a coma and was later diagnosed with diabetes. Now, at twenty, his diabetes made him eligible for career counseling and financial aid from the Bureau of Vocational Rehabilitation. There, he discovered how much his barbering was really a way of appeasing our father. He decided to change his career to electronics, which had always interested him. With his high school degree, he could enroll in a two-year degree program in instrumentation electronics at the West Side Institute of Technology.

After completing his studies there, he was employed as a salesman and trouble-shooter for a company that manufactured steel additives for steel mills. The company had customers all over the country which required Tom to fly frequently. With his barbering days over and a new and promising career ahead, Tom stopped seeking help from his spiritual power altogether. Without its vital presence, he was unprepared for the life-threatening crisis that lay ahead of him.

While at the technical institute he met Betty, whom he married in 1975. I never knew her well and could hardly recall the wedding. By then, I was living in Minnesota and came home only for occasional visits. Though Tom and I respected and liked each other, we were no longer in touch.

No one in our family was aware Betty had a serious addiction problem, abusing prescription drugs and shooting heroin. Though Tom's work often took him out of town, he knew of Betty's drug problem. However, he minimized the seriousness of it and made half-hearted attempts at controlling her behavior by refusing to allow her to shoot heroin in front of him. For a year, Betty tried to keep her use of drugs out of Tom's sight, but she eventually abandoned any pretense and shot heroin at home whether Tom was in the room or not. He did nothing to intervene. Though her dependence on him made him feel needed, he wasn't able to help her. In time, he too began to drink heavily. Drug dealers who supplied Betty eventually showed up at their apartment, and though Tom never dealt in drugs, he allowed them into his home. Two other young women, one of them a prostitute and topless dancer, moved in to live with Tom and his wife. By then, Tom could no longer control what happened in his own apartment. One day, a male acquaintance of one of the women was murdered on their front steps. Hoping to get a "fresh start" and salvage their own relationship, Tom and Betty moved into another apartment. It was too late, and soon afterwards they divorced.

Depression was Tom's albatross, and he quickly slipped back into his gloom. He no longer maintained his diabetic diet. Soon after leaving Betty, he was hospitalized for a week with pneumonia. "I was so sick I couldn't eat or drink," he said. "I wasn't thinking about my friend, the Positive Force. I never thought about it anymore. For years I didn't even ask my old God for help. It never crossed my mind to ask for help. I might have if I had remembered."

After recovering, he returned to work. He continued to fly all over the United States and Canada, visiting steel mills to repair automated equipment, until an accident set off a series of catastrophes that led him to his ultimate crisis.

After being given clearance into a restricted area to pick up tools, he drove a rental car over an I-beam that was buried in the mud. The car was extensively damaged, and he was promptly sued by the rental company. To avoid being drawn into the suit, the company fired Tom for operating a motor vehicle in an unauthorized area.

A few weeks later, he was driving along when he suddenly saw out of one eye what looked like thick black syrup spilling over a TV screen. Within minutes that eye went blind from hemorrhaging caused by his diabetes.

He drove home, relying on one eye, and called the doctor, who explained that nothing could be done about his eyesight. Tom hung up the phone. He sat in the chair and imagined never recovering his sight. He imagined his other eye hemorrhaging and leaving him totally blind. How would he cook, drive a car, dress himself, or even walk around the block? His fear of blindness compounded the fear of poverty he had after losing his job. He felt hopeless. Then, the phone rang. It was the brother of his ex-wife Betty calling from Denver to notify Tom that Betty had shot herself in the head. Stunned, Tom listened as the brother explained how Betty's heroin addiction led her into prostitution and then to suicide.

Tom hung up the phone and cried. Within one month he was sued, fired from his job, had gone blind in one eye, and now his ex-wife was dead. He considered walking to the corner bar, but getting drunk would only offer him temporary relief. Once again, the ultimate escape came to mind. He put on his jacket and drove to Sam's Pro Golf shop where he bought a .38 handgun and a box of hollow-point bullets.

Without help from his personal transcendent power, Tom had resorted to his old belief that God was punishing him for his sins. "I figured God was doing all that to me. I had no chance if I had to pay for everything I did." God again loomed like a menacing ghost in a child's room about to lurch out of a closet to devour him. His failure to maintain his spiritual fitness made him a victim of his own tortuous beliefs.

Tom returned to his apartment and lay on his bed. He watched himself in the dresser mirror, exploring the deadliest angle at which to insert the gun into his mouth. He practiced pulling the trigger before loading the gun. To guarantee that no one would hear the shot and save him, he decided to use a pillow to muffle the sound. He carefully adjusted it so the spark from the hammer wouldn't set the pillow on fire, endangering others in the apartment house. Tom then loaded a single bullet, cocked the pistol, and opened his mouth.

He slowly began to squeeze the trigger. "I felt the trigger move," he said, when he had a sudden revelation that God did not exist. He lay absolutely still, loosened his finger on the trigger, and took the gun out of his mouth.

"I felt relieved that no God existed to punish me," Tom said. He put the gun down, got up from the bed and called a friend.

He told his friend about his attempted suicide, and most importantly how he now realized that there was no punishing God, no ghost in his dark room. It was an illumination that dispelled not God, but his demon. He felt this insight turned on a light in his consciousness that was now strong enough to keep him from taking his life when nothing else could. Since it wasn't God afflicting him, he told his friend, perhaps he had brought on his own troubles. That possibility gave Tom the hope he desperately needed. "At least I had a chance," he said. His rejection of what he thought was God cleansed Tom of self-destructive beliefs and prepared him for a more significant revelation.

His friend immediately arranged an appointment for him with a psychologist.

The next day, in the therapist's office, Tom was asked if there was ever a time when God was a healing force in his life. Was there ever a loving being greater than himself available to help him?

"I told her that the only God I had was bearded, wore a white robe, and wasn't good for me," Tom replied. "But I suddenly remembered the morning outside the delicatessen years ago." Tom was now thirty-three years old. He spent the entire hour discussing the experience with his therapist.

When Tom left the therapist's office, he took the elevator down to the ground floor and pushed open the heavy glass doors to leave the building. As he stepped outside and began walking down the steps, he suddenly found himself as though in a time warp. He experienced being at two places at once: outside the delicatessen near the barber shop in 1968 and outside the therapist's office in 1983.

"The air smelled the same. And I could smell the exhaust of the cars, though I didn't see any cars outside the office building. I was back there in 1968 and outside the therapist's office building simultaneously. It wasn't just deja vu. I could actually hear the cars on Denison Avenue and feel the same warm sun on my face outside the therapist's office. I knew where I really was, but I was also back in the past. It was uncanny. I could see the colors, the red poster on the window at the deli. I was standing in front of the store again, yet...."

As often occurs in mystical experiences, Tom's past and present connected in a single moment.

Though physical similarities between the two places existed, both being industrial, it was a deeper spiritual dimension that connected the two locations and the two times. For Tom, each place informed and deepened the meaning of the other. The sacred moment and the Force Tom experienced in 1968 now reappeared to him in the present as God.

"When I walked outside, I knew that I had a God. I smiled then as I had while walking back to the barber school. I had a sense of gratitude." As Tom sat across from me, tears came to his eyes. "I knew that I had God back in 1968, only I didn't completely realize it. That other God, the punishing one, didn't exist. He was never there, only in my mind. That's when I think I had a spiritual experience because I finally knew that the 'Force' was actually God."

The gratitude Tom felt on both occasions is with him even to this day. "I never felt anything like that since. Now I take God with me. Now I can achieve an understanding of God of my own choosing. It is a positive energy that doesn't care if you do something bad. Then, it just isn't around. When it is by you, it helps. I'll have God in the car with me, floating there, and I'll talk out loud to Him, asking about our dad." Sometimes, Tom feels loved by our father as he is loved by God.

When Tom experienced the loving presence of God he also discovered the presence of our father like a guardian spirit in his life. Perhaps Tom had projected his relationship with our father onto God, which accounted for his belief in a punishing deity. Tom remembered our dad calling him "stupid," and he resented him for that and other reasons. Tom had a much more troubled relationship with our father than I did. When Tom spoke his resentments towards him, I wanted to come to my father's defense. But I was here with Tom as a witness, not a judge.

I asked Tom if he had to heal his relationship with our dad before he could experience a loving heavenly Father or God. He didn't think so. It wasn't our dad, he said, that led him to God. "It was God who led me back to Dad."

Today, Tom believes a man must keep himself open and receptive to spiritual experience. "You have to quit struggling and not care if anyone ever likes you, not care what happens...total surrender and total defeat. I'm here and I don't give a damn....After I gave up, I had my experience.

"It's harder for men to surrender," Tom adds. "They are more controlled. If men would talk about it, they would understand. It has to be a man-to-man type of thing because men intuitively understand the feelings of other men without hearing them."

Tom is convinced that a man needs to do two things for his spiritual life: realize that he needs help and ask for that help. Tom prays and meditates daily so he won't forget to ask—and say thanks.

He has gone from spiritual rags to riches, from being a juvenile delinquent and thief to an outstanding member of his community. Once truant from school, flunking every subject, Tom recently graduated with honors from Baldwin Wallace College in Berea, Ohio, and may attend graduate school in business. He is often contacted by others to intervene in emergencies with youths who are delinquent or suicidal. He is now happily married and has a stepson. Often, he volunteers himself for medical research in diabetes.

The support and recognition he receives from friends and our family is exemplary. I *do* speak for everyone in our family when I say Tom is the most loving and caring man we know. His inner work not only heals himself, but the entire family. Once a source of worry and grief for us, he is now a source of joy and wonder. What he does for himself he does for all of us—not just for his family, but for society too. I'm sure our dad is in the afterlife, pointing Tom out to everyone, saying, "That's my son!"

When I shut off the tape recorder that summer afternoon, I felt relieved, exhausted, grateful, and joyful. In the hours we talked on the front porch, Tom had shown me his very soul, his most intimate self. Shared, his sacred moments had brought us together as brothers often hope to be in their lives. I had no trouble calling his sacred moments religious experiences though he rarely attended church. His experience was not only a bond between him and God, but now a bond between brother and brother, keepers of each others' joys and sufferings.

CHAPTER 7

A Hundred Feet
High

The soul is just as safe in its body as in the
Kingdom of Heaven.

— Mechthild of Magdeburg

Every Sunday morning when Wayne was a boy he
reluctantly dressed in the clothes his mother had
laid out the night before. He disliked wearing the
hot and itchy tweed trousers, the white shirt stiff
from starch and ironing, the tight black shoes, and
the bow tie under his chin. Like many boys his age,
Wayne preferred old shirts and pants, even school
clothes, to his oppressive Sunday attire.

After he dressed and ate breakfast, he and his
four sisters and two brothers walked twelve blocks

with his parents to a Baptist church. No matter what the weather, his mother pushed a large buggy with his two younger siblings inside. Plastic was draped over the buggy to keep the babies dry if it rained.

Every Sunday, Wayne spent two hours in the morning and evening at church. Even during the afternoons at home, his father would persuade Wayne to read from the Bible by offering him twenty-five cents for any book of the Bible he read. As he'd read in the living room, his father followed along in his own Bible. "I had to real aloud because he didn't trust me," he said. "He made sure I read every word and didn't skip anything. For a while I thought it was a good deal. I could read pretty fast and make a quarter a book." Soon though, Wayne tired of reading, and not even twenty-five cents was worth sacrificing an hour of play time.

Wayne remembered the day when his father found Jesus, was anointed with oil by an old Baptist minister, and soon afterward began scolding Wayne for his sins. He was skeptical of his father's faith. "You had to believe his religion if you wanted any attention or affection from him, and I didn't," he said.

By the time he was ten, Wayne's rebellion against religious fundamentalism was under way. He would sneak out of church during Sunday morning service and take his twenty-five cents collection money to a restaurant two blocks away. At first he worried that "God would come through the roof" to punish him for spending the money on pop and candy bars. But in a short while Wayne got braver and began going to the movie theater next door to the church instead of the restaurant. Admission to the movies in 1947 was only twelve cents, which left him with change for candy. Though members of the congregation had reported Wayne's absences, his parents had given up trying to control him.

Normally his father insisted on absolute obedience enforced with physical beatings. Whenever the children misbehaved, all Wayne's mother had to say was, "Wait till you father gets home," and they'd stop whatever they were doing. When Wayne's father arrived home, he would often beat the children with a razor strap. "In time, all he had to do was make the strap pop in the air," Wayne said. The sound of the belt snapping above their heads was enough to make them behave.

One evening the entire family sat at the kitchen table waiting for Mr. Neilson to select a biblical passage to read before supper. Wayne's cousin, Tim, was living with them then. They had taken him in as a foster child after the boy's father had died and his mother had given Tim up to the state. Tim was crippled with club feet.

As Mr. Neilson thumbed through the Bible to select a reading, the children bowed their heads and waited. But Tim was distracted, looking outside the kitchen window to the pigeon coop he had built. Like many eleven-year-olds, Tim was more concerned with his hobby than his prayers. He was especially sensitive to anyone insulting his pigeons by calling them "scrubs," a term comparable to calling a pedigreed dog a mongrel.

Mr. Neilson looked up from his Bible to see Tim staring out the window. "Don't scrub, let's pray," his father said. The comment was intended to warn Tim to pay attention to the prayers not the pigeons, but Wayne, along with everyone else at the table, thought it funny and laughed. Mr. Neilson went into a rage and shouted at them all to stop laughing. He rose from his chair and went to each one at the table. "Did you laugh?" he asked. As each of his children confessed, he slapped them. "You better hit me too because I laughed." his wife said. Mr. Neilson's hand suddenly opened and struck her across the face.

"He was a big man and nearly knocked us off our chairs," Wayne said. "We were used to it, but to hit Mother was unforgivable." The children regarded her as a saint, and for a long time no one talked to Mr. Neilson. The supper incident fueled Wayne's resentment. He hated listening to his father read from Revelations. In Wayne's mind, the beast in Revelations was not Satan or the Antichrist, but his father. "I think my father had a psychic break, not a religious experience," he said.

Though the regimen of attending church for four hours every Sunday was partially relieved for Wayne by sneaking out, there were other obligations he couldn't escape. On Wednesdays he had to attend prayer meetings and on Friday nights Missionary Society. During the summer Wayne went on trips with his family to the church's camp near Snail Lake. There, he stood on the lake's shore with the congregation while a young woman or man dressed entirely in white stood in the water alongside the minister. Wayne sang half-heartedly with the rest as the minister leaned the participant back in his arm as if dipping a partner in a dance and immersed the initiate into the water for baptism. All Wayne's siblings were baptized in Snail Lake. "The other kids went along," Wayne said. He was the only one who rebelled.

Tent meetings were also scheduled during the summer. Sawdust usually covered the ground and folding chairs were set up under the tent. Wayne sat and witnessed many "altar calls" of the people who'd suddenly spring up from their chairs and walk up the aisle after being called by Jesus to repent. They'd kneel at a platform while others laid hands over them and prayed. Wayne disliked the crying and emotional fervor.

The only way Wayne saw to escape his fundamental religious upbringing and his father's tyranny was to run away from home. The first time he ran away he was only eight.

"For some reason, my friend Billy and I were angry at our fathers and we decided to run away," Wayne said. They left early one school morning on their bikes. Because of his family's poverty, Wayne couldn't afford a new one and his was assembled from a collection of parts from other bikes. The boys rode along the railroad bed that paralleled the main road so as not to be seen. As they pedaled to a cabin Billy's father owned fifteen miles from home, they imagined themselves free to do as they pleased. They would live off the fat of the land in the wilderness. Wayne would never have to go to church or listen to his father rave about sin.

It took them all morning to reach the cabin that they thought would be stocked with food and fishing gear. When they swung open the door, they found the cabin empty of gear. It had been closed for the season. Only one can of chicken noodle soup was in the cupboard. There was no electricity nor any kerosene for the lanterns. As night came, the hoots of owls and other sounds from the woods frightened the boys. It was after one in the morning when their fathers arrived and took them back home. Wayne felt partly relieved.

Having come so close to his freedom, Wayne became increasingly intolerant of his home life. By the time he turned fourteen, he had run away three more times. "After a while they didn't even look for me," he said. Two years later, his father kicked him out of the house for good. Wayne would come home only when his father was at work. Then, his mother fed him and washed his clothes. He never knew the acceptance and safety that home was supposed to offer children.

When he finished high school, Wayne joined the Air Force, married, and later moved to Seattle to live with his Uncle Jake. He could remember his uncle bouncing him on his knee as a child and letting him sip from his beer glass. Uncle Jake had always given Wayne Christmas presents, and as a semi-pro boxer Jake often delighted Wayne with boxing stories. Jake had lost two fingers at a work accident and would amuse Wayne with finger tricks. He would jab Wayne with his stump, and the boy loved it. Most importantly, Jake never pressured Wayne on religious matters.

Jake was a welder. As a member of Seattle's Boilermakers Union, he got Wayne an apprenticeship in a shipyard. Wayne worked hard every day alongside his mentor. At night he attended classes at Seattle Community College for five years until he finished his apprenticeship and was licensed as a construction boilermaker. Now he could be employed to build refineries and tanks in oil fields, stacks, towers, storage vessels for liquid nitrogen, barges, boats, and bridges.

By 1968, when Wayne was thirty-one, he had a wife and three children. His family obligations pressured him to look for better work. Then, oil refineries in Alaska were luring young men north with the promise of good money and glamorous work in the woods. As a licensed journeyman, the most skilled of all boilermakers, Wayne was sought by the refineries because he could do all aspects of the trade: high rigging, riveting, chipping, welding, and ship-fitting. Wayne left his family in Seattle and set out that spring for the Kenai Peninsula, 180 miles west of Anchorage on the Cook Inlet.

Wayne was to build storage tanks for offshore oil drilling rigs. For the first month, he did mostly what he called gopher work, simple but strenuous tasks usually assigned to new men on the job. He was exhausted and afraid that he lacked the stamina to go on.

The physical stress of the work was intensified by Wayne's fear of not being able to do it. One of the hardest and most dangerous jobs was throwing scaffolding. He had to pitch green timber planks that weren't cured, which made them much heavier with sap. Each plank was about two and a half inches thick, twelve inches wide, and up to twenty feet long. A man had to literally throw them up from one level to the next. Wayne balanced the beams on his arm, and, using centrifugal force, swung them up to the next level. One day Wayne swung a beam up but it didn't quite reach the man and came back down at him like a javelin, crashing a hundred feet below. No one was hurt, but there were plenty of other mishaps. Some men fell forty or fifty feet and were badly hurt. Wayne knew one of those men. "He was so crippled up they finally kept him on the ground.

"It's a lot of work to pretend all the time," he said, describing how the men hid their fears. "You had to act tough. Even if you were feeling horseshit and scared, you pretended you weren't. Sometimes they hung sheets of steel that were forty feet long, ten feet wide, and a half inch thick. They were hung by two hooks from a crane that swung them in the air and put them in place. That was a really scary moment when they did that. If the wind caught that great big shield, it would take off like a sail on a boat. More than once it went crashing through the tank. If you didn't get out of the way, you were cut in half.

"You could never say to another guy, 'Boy, that

scared the shit out of me.' Instead, you'd blame the rigger or crane operator and say, 'What's wrong with that dumb son of a bitch down there?' That was okay. You could never say, 'I'm really frightened.' Alaska was Macho Land. You didn't talk about personal things, not even sex unless it was a joke."

There were more frightening dangers. Occasionally, the men used foot-long steel pins which tapered from a two inch diameter head to a point like an ordinary pin. Some of these were intentionally dropped on certain men below who were disliked for one reason or another. "Once they threw the pins at a man in a pickup truck and dented the top. They scared the hell out of that guy," Wayne said.

Often Wayne had to fasten one end of a rope to the peak of a domed tank with the other end tied around his waist. He lowered and raised himself on the rope to grind off welds and smooth seams. On windy days, Wayne often wasn't sure whether he'd live to see the end of the work day.

"I had never done anything like that, so it was really scary for me. It was a tense and stressful job. I wasn't in very good shape. The job was in a camp with all men. Across the street was a roadhouse—a bar, motel, and cafe with live music, dancing, drinking, and gambling—and that's where everyone went. We worked seven days a week, ten hours a day and spent six hours in the roadhouse drinking and eating. There was a lot of fighting. I was afraid people might think I wasn't a real man. Plus, I was tired of being lonely."

His marriage wasn't going well. His wife often wrote him and complained that he wasn't sending enough money for her and his three children. Wayne admitted he was hiding money from her. "I got a dollar vacation pay for every hour I worked and didn't tell her."

His work conditions, the imminence of danger, his lack of stamina, his deteriorating relationship with his wife, and peer pressure all contributed to Wayne's turmoil. In part, his situation in Alaska strangely resembled the family situation he thought he had escaped when he was seventeen. He felt threatened physically and emotionally in both situations, and his need for reassurance and safety were paramount.

Early one morning, after skipping breakfast, he arrived at the work site at five. No one had yet arrived. The usual crash and bang of tools, sledge hammers whacked against steel tanks, the roar of fifty-ton cranes, and the shouts and curses of workmen hadn't begun. Wayne especially enjoyed the half hour silence before the men arrived. Wearing his heavy leather welding jacket, he began his climb up the tank ladder. As every morning at that hour, the tide was running out. The Kenai Peninsula had one of the highest tides in the world. "Nearly thirty-two feet," Wayne said. "I could actually see it. If there were pilings they formed a wake because the water goes out so fast as far as you can see. I had some kind of thing with tides. I can't describe how watching the tide made me feel."

Sitting at the top of the tank over a hundred feet above the ground, Wayne was at the highest point in the area and could see for miles. He felt safe there. "It was the one place I could go and be by myself. I didn't have to worry about people putting me down," he said. Woods and water stretched as far as he could imagine. The tops of pine and fir trees, discolored from the lack of sunlight, spread a yellowish brown blanket over the land. "I guess you could say I was meditating, but I didn't know what the word 'meditating' meant at the time. I was just being by myself."

As he gazed out into the woods, a moose and its two calves suddenly appeared below him. Because the animals couldn't see Wayne high above them, the animals lingered in the open area. "The cow, the female moose, had no horns and was all head," Wayne said. "The calves were gangly, all legs and wobbly. The cow was eating and the calves were following her. I don't know what it was—the tide going out, the silence, or the animals—but all of a sudden, I wasn't alone. I felt a sense of belonging and connection. The animals were my friends. It's hard to explain because it's all inside. It must be what happens when a flower blooms, goes from a bud and all of a sudden it opens up," Wayne said, pointing to his chest. "Suddenly I'm like a blooming rose, a flower for a short time.

"Something had made it okay, because I hadn't done anything. Everything would work out. A part of it was a feeling of safety. I didn't have to prove myself. I had a lot of trouble in my life feeling like I belonged anywhere, but for that moment on the dome I didn't have to worry about anything. I felt I was free, and I was stepping on air."

Was there an infusion of knowledge or rare insight? "No, I had more of a sense that I didn't have to know anything. I knew enough. I knew whatever I needed to know. I just felt really connected. At peace."

Wayne experienced the same peace and exalted consciousness on two other occasions in his life. Seventeen years after his experience on the dome in Alaska, Wayne had been divorced and had custody of his twelve-year-old daughter from a second marriage. She had accompanied Wayne on a fishing trip to Big Lake, but was still asleep in the cabin that morning. It was summer and the lake was calm.

The sun hadn't yet risen over the water. Wayne and a close friend had gotten up early, eaten breakfast, and filled the thermos with coffee before leaving the cabin to load fishing gear into a boat. The two men knew from the previous day where northern pike were biting and after loading the boat motored directly to the spot.

As they trolled the waters, Wayne spotted a pair of loons, male and female, with two babies. The male was characteristically colored with black and white feathers. Their early morning cries were haunting and at first gave Wayne a feeling of sadness. But as the sun rose over the horizon of water, the loon cries seemed more natural as they dipped and dove into the water for food.

"The adults kept their bodies between us and the baby loons. All of a sudden I felt overwhelmed. It's hard to explain. I've fished a lot in my life but at that moment it was really powerful. It was similar to the feeling at the top of the dome. I felt the same feeling of being well, on the right path. I felt I was related to those loons or something. Some kind of a crazy thing like that. They were a part of me or I was a part of them. I'm not sure. We were all part of a much bigger thing, as if we were all a part of a big painting."

Wayne glanced at his friend in the boat. "I could tell by just looking at him he didn't feel it at all. He was busy fussing with the motor and looking into his tackle box. I didn't say anything. It was my thing, and it would be spoiled if I said anything to him. It lasted for a while, like a meditation."

Wayne's frequent use of the pronoun "it" to describe the sensation of bliss and union with nature makes clear how ineffable the moment was for him. "It" had no name, no language.

The moment on the lake was a spiritual one for Wayne because "everything made sense. I don't find that feeling in church. A lot of times I feel pessimistic about life—that it's all a crock. But at that moment watching the loons, life seemed exciting, important, and right. That's why it's spiritual. I suddenly knew I was part of things. I wasn't all alone. I felt like I had a soul.

"Fishing is more than just fishing to me," he said. "I'll go fishing by myself sometimes. I kind of seek out the moment on the dome or the peace with the loons." Fishing was also a way for Wayne to be more intimate with men. "For most women I know, to sit in a boat all day long and get dirty, stinky, and hot is not a spiritual experience. But I feel real good inside, real connected to the other man. I probably haven't said anything much to him, haven't talked over anything heavy. It isn't fishing so much or talking, but just being together in the silence. Then, I feel really good."

Months after Wayne's fishing experience, he had a third spiritual experience in the midst of a tragic event in his life. His son was twenty-four years old, a race car mechanic, and had just broken off his engagement to a woman who had left him to date other men. The day after New Year's, he was speeding down a mountain highway in New Mexico with his best friend when he lost control of the car, careened off the road, and crashed into a boulder. The two young men were killed instantly.

"When my son was killed, I was in shock. I had to go to a department store to pick out clothes to bury him in. I had my two daughters with me to help. I was crying." Because his son preferred blue jeans, Wayne and his daughters decided against buying a suit. Instead, they bought a sweater, slacks, and a dress shirt to bury him in. Wayne recalled even buying a belt, underwear, socks, and shoes.

Afterward, as they left the store and crossed the parking lot, Wayne's daughters walked ahead of him. "Like a flash, all of a sudden this thing happened to me." Just before they reached their car, Wayne experienced his son's presence. "I knew my son was okay. Before that I was really upset, shocked, and confused. But then I knew he was somewhere, and it was okay. I didn't know where. I didn't know how I knew that, I just knew. I don't conceptualize heaven, but I knew he was safe."

His brief moment in the parking lot gave Wayne a reassurance that he would never lose. Like the moments on the dome and in the fishing boat, he experienced a profound emotional certitude that would forever remind him of what he sought in his daily life. Though Wayne didn't articulate any particular knowledge of God, everything clicked. Like a lock being opened, the tumblers fell into place at those moments and a treasured serenity was revealed. "Something was watching over me," Wayne said. "I have a higher power that has evolved into a friend, but it's hard to explain that stuff."

Wayne's sacred moments critically shaped his spiritual life. Prior to his first moment on the dome, his experience of God was largely determined by his father. God was a punishing and wrathful tyrant. After he left home and recovered from his father's detrimental influence, he had no more use for that God, and subsequently God became the Inessential Being, a Nothingness. The combined effect of his three sacred moments helped him to finally transform God from Nothing to Friend, and this transformation marks his spiritual evolution. Alfred North Whitehead described this evolution in three stages: first, experiencing God as Void, second as Enemy, and finally as "God the companion." For Wayne, God as companion or friend didn't simply mean best buddy or pal but presence, love, and support.

Wayne's spiritual experiences tell him "there is something sacred in my life. I have a spiritual connection and I can't label it very well. There's a knowledge inside me that everything is okay. Those experiences have given me the serenity I have in my life. I have a better sense of who I am because I realize I do have a spiritual life. I have something going besides just who I appear to be. Those moments are keys to that."

Not until twelve years after his first sacred moment did Wayne make dramatic changes. Nevertheless, by 1980 he began to deal with a drinking problem developed in Alaska, left his job as a boilermaker, went to court and got custody of his daughter, then seven years old, returned to college, and began working with the disabled.

He now has college degrees in human services and chemical dependency, with special emphasis on the elderly and disabled. In addition, he does volunteer work, with three separate agencies, in hospices.

Wayne still guards his sacred moments and rarely confides them to anyone. "I don't think anybody would understand. I never ran into anybody who had similar experiences. One reason I wouldn't share it is because someone might laugh at me and

I would never take that risk." Twelve years after the dome experience, he spoke to a man in Seattle about it. "It was unsatisfying. He liked me and listened, but he didn't know what I was talking about. He just said, 'oh, that was interesting.'"

When asked if he thought he'd be able to speak to a clergy member about his spiritual experiences, Wayne winced. "I have trouble talking to clergy about anything. I feel judged. That religious stuff I don't believe or understand or accept. I sort of stick my head into the sand and don't pay any attention to it."

Yet Wayne acknowledges having a need to connect with a community of people for the purpose of affirming his faith. "I've made efforts to join a church. I know I need something inside to make me more complete. Religion hasn't given it to me, but music and fishing does."

Wayne will occasionally attend church, but never any particular one for more than six months. "I am not committed to any one church, but I'm committed to gaining more spirituality. I enjoy the people, the music, going with my friends." The church he now attends is "into real things, like helping the homeless." For him, a church must advocate either a liberal theology or actively respond to social issues to have any lasting value. "They turned their parish house into a hospice for the dying," he said. He also likes the church's music, which occasionally features a violinist, and the congregation has older members he enjoys talking to. Wayne said attending church is "something social, but I don't get my peace there.

"Maybe church is more about me accepting them. But I just can't accept the whole package." He gave the example of receiving communion as something he couldn't accept. "I think it's barbaric, drinking Jesus' blood and eating His body. So I don't take communion, but I feel funny sitting in my chair, isolated. There are many rows of people behind me who can see me sitting all alone." Though Wayne hopes to share his spirituality with others, it's ironic that communion, which underscores community in many churches, alienates him.

One might think Wayne would be more welcomed in evangelical churches than in the traditional mainstream churches that he now occasionally attends. Certainly, his father and members of the church would rejoice in hearing his testimony of a religious experience on top of an oil tank. But Wayne didn't believe he'd find any more acceptance there than in a more traditional church. "I wasn't born again," he said. His understanding of the "Friend" was radically different from his father's understanding of Jesus.

Sacred moments aren't common experiences

that people readily discuss, like grocery shopping or even divorce, where people may more easily identify and say, "Oh yeah, that happened to me, too." It's understandable that Wayne wants his most cherished experiences acceptable to others, to share them, but he can't expect others to readily embrace those experiences as he has. The only place Wayne can be sure of finding acceptance of his spiritual life is within himself. There, the sacred moment exists authentically and most convincingly, "like a blooming rose, a flower."

CHAPTER 8

Absolutely No Drugs or Alcohol beyond This Point

Sometimes I can feel the peace right here in my chest where the knot used to be.

— Bob

Middletown, Iowa, where Bob and Marlene lived, was a quiet town in 1972 with a population of less than five hundred people. All the children went to the town's only school, and on Saturdays they played in the streets without much concern for traffic or strangers. Everyone in Middletown knew each other. On Saturdays, people chatted and exchanged news and gossip at the local grocery store where everyone shopped. Located in southern Iowa, the town sprung up around the Iowa Army Ammunition Plant where many of the townspeople worked.

Bob was thirty-four years old and had worked at the plant as a computer analyst for twelve years. "The plant was a branch of the Atomic Energy Commission," he said. "We assembled atomic bombs."

Every morning when Bob arrived at work, he had his briefcase inspected by an armed guard stationed at the main entrance. A large sign lettered in black above the entrance read, "Absolutely No Drugs or Alcohol beyond This Point." And every morning, Bob walked past the sign with tranquilizers and vodka concealed inside his coat pockets.

During his lunch hour, Bob frequently left work and did not return until two or three hours later. He often sat in his car in the parking lot, swigging from his bottle of vodka, taking tranquilizers, and gazing dumbly out the window. Many days, he called in sick when he was hung over. He missed weeks of work because of hospitalizations for his deteriorating health. The ammunition plant tolerated Bob's erratic behavior for years until January 1972 when he was forced to resign to avoid being fired.

It was ironic that Bob worked in a nuclear plant where armed guards and electronic detection devices were stationed at various locations to protect the plant from sabotage or unauthorized personnel. No one suspected Bob or realized that through drug and alcohol addiction Bob had lost his soul. He was the equivalent of a terrorist, a walking time bomb. At the Iowa Army Ammunition Plant where national security was paramount, Bob had no personal or spiritual security.

Bob, Marlene, and their two children lived on Alexander Avenue, one of the few streets that made up the town. Their three-bedroom, two-story frame house wasn't much different from the rest of the homes on Alexander. They did have apple trees and mock orange bushes in the yard. The trees were nearly ready to blossom that afternoon on St. Patrick's Day when an ambulance sped along Highway 34 to Bob and Marlene's house.

That morning Bob had gotten up as usual before his wife, slipped on his bathrobe, and walked downstairs to the basement. There, he took out two cans of beer from the basement refrigerator and sat on an old broken rocking chair with a child's guard rail laid across the seat for a cushion. He laid a towel over the top of the beer can so his wife wouldn't hear its pop. With his first swig he washed down two 500 milligram capsules of chloral hydrate. Soon after he finished the beer, he vomited into the sewer drain.

That morning was no different from any other. Bob started each morning by taking a "Mickey

Finn," a few drops of the chloral hydrate we've seen on television secretly poured into someone's drink to knock them out.

As he swigged from his second beer, he stared out the small basement window, a peephole into an incomprehensible world. He waited to be numbed by a dose of chloral hydrate that might have knocked another man unconscious. His doctor had prescribed the drug instead of sleeping pills as a sedative because Bob's liver, deteriorated from hepatitis and jaundice, couldn't easily metabolize or absorb sleeping pills. Chloral hydrate was much easier on the liver and was the only medication that could quiet the beast in him. "I can't live fully awake," Bob might have said before taking his Mickey Finn each morning. One could hardly imagine a man more desperate and doomed.

Despite Bob's attempt to muffle the fizz of beer, his wife lay awake upstairs in bed, listening to Bob in the basement. The sounds traveled easily through the otherwise quiet house. "I'd be laying in bed and the first thing I'd hear was the tops of the beer cans opening. A few minutes later I'd hear him vomiting," she said.

That morning Bob had secretly decided to make one last pitiful effort to turn back the darkening tide threatening to engulf him. He waited until late afternoon when his wife was preparing supper and his two children were playing outside to leave the house. No one noticed him gone.

To be outside alone for any length of time terrified Bob. Besides suffering from alcoholism he also had agoraphobia, a fear of open places. To take a short walk around the town's two blocks, past the grocery store, the post office, and gas station required a Promethean effort. Only halfway up the street, Bob began mulling over what the psychiatrist had said the day before to Marlene: "He's not trying." The psychiatrist suggested that Marlene take the kids and leave Bob. The thought panicked him. She was the only one who took care of him.

On reaching the end of his street, Bob had arrived at the border of a full-blown break with reality. Though it was a cool afternoon, his blood was rushing through his body, flushing his face, and causing him to sweat and tremble. Panic throbbed in his chest and he mentally blacked out. "My mind quit functioning," Bob said. "I don't remember anything beyond that point."

He had stepped into a nightmare that took him from one terrifying scene to the next without any logical connection. He suddenly found himself lying in a copse of bushes without any explanation or memory of stumbling. His face was scratched and cut. Blood trickled from his forehead and cheek. He struggled to get back up only to fall again. The next thing he remembered was opening the front door of a neighbor's house and walking in. Then suddenly he was lying on the neighbor's living room floor and didn't know why a man, weighing over 200 pounds, was sitting on top of him. Bob drooled, shook, and thrashed on the carpet.

Marlene came running to the house after the neighbor had called her on the phone. "Bob was in stark terror," she said, "like a caged animal." Marlene managed to take him home and call the local hospital.

Alerted by the siren, neighbors came out and stood on their porches to watch as the ambulance pulled into the driveway and two medics stepped out. Across the street, Bob's two young children watched through a neighbor's window as the medics entered their house and within minutes brought their father out on the gurney.

"Please, don't use the siren unless you have to," Marlene pleaded with the driver as she climbed into the cab. She feared the blast of the siren would only panic her husband more.

A few blocks from the hospital Bob started gagging on his own saliva and gasped for air. The driver then turned on the siren and accelerated toward the emergency room. At the hospital Bob was tranquilized and a nurse accompanied him and the medics to the state institution at Mount Pleasant.

Once there, the medics swung open the back doors of the ambulance and prepared to take Bob out. Marlene leaned over him to kiss him goodbye when he reached for her hand. "This time we're going to make it," he said. But Bob had already had four hospitalizations, and there was no evidence that this time would be any different.

He was admitted to a locked drug and alcohol unit. "I had my very own padded cell, and I think mattresses were on the walls. They had a cot in it and one little window in the door that looked out into the hallway. When I looked out there was a guy standing outside the door peeing on the floor. I remember itching terribly."

Bob was in a locked unit with patients who suffered from "wet brain" as a result of long-term alcoholism. Bob's health had severely deteriorated from chronic abuse of alcohol, tranquilizers, sleeping pills, and antidepressants. He had drug-induced hepatitis and jaundice. His liver had swollen and protruded. His gall bladder was no longer functioning and he had an overactive thyroid. Physically, emotionally, and spiritually, Bob was nearly dead.

After seven weeks in the locked unit, he was transferred to an open unit where he could wear his own clothes, attend group sessions, see movies, and socialize in the lounge. He had shown much improvement, and the hospital staff began preparing Bob for his discharge. But Bob knew he would return to his life of destruction the moment he left the hospital. The thought of leaving panicked him. Though he was permitted and encouraged to walk around the hospital grounds, Bob hadn't yet exercised that privilege.

"I couldn't walk out of the hospital because the panic and fear would hit. I didn't want to leave the place. I couldn't make it on the outside. I would rather they cut off both my arms and legs than let me out. I thought I could stay in Mount Pleasant. The only option I had was to kill myself or someone else. I really thought that once I got to Mount Pleasant I was where I belonged, and I was going to be there for the rest of my life."

One afternoon, anxious about his discharge, Bob retired to his room while other patients chatted in the lounge. The room was sparsely furnished with only a sink, a chair and table, two cots, and a window that overlooked another building. He shut the door and lay in his bunk.

As many seriously ill patients do, Bob feebly bargained with God as he lay in bed. "I talked out loud." I said, 'God, if you're up there, please help me. If you help me, I will try to do the best I can for the rest of my life to help other people.'"

Bob could hardly help himself, let alone other people. He had often promised God and his wife that he would mend his ways and stop drinking. He was no more able at that moment than at any previous time to follow through with his part of the bargain. But for some inexplicable reason, Bob suddenly found himself in the midst of a spiritual experience.

"It happened suddenly. I felt like I was apart from myself. I could see a baby being held on God's right shoulder. I didn't know how I knew it was God; I just did. The baby was held with his head on the shoulder, patted, and reassured. As I was watching this, I could feel it happening to me. I could see this small child being held and knew it was me. I was apart from it, yet was in it. I could feel His arms around me and feel the pressure of His hands on my back. God had picked me up and held me like the little baby."

Bob's sacred moment was remarkable for its childlike qualities. While many men might refuse to yield to the moment and say no to the thought of identifying with the baby, Bob immersed himself in his vision of what he had already become: helpless, needy, like a little baby. By descending more fully into what he must have resisted for a long time, he could be healed by his surrender. Now, Bob could surrender to God, admit his defeat, and allow himself to be reassured as a child in loving arms.

"I don't know how long it lasted. It could have lasted for a second or ten minutes. I don't remember how it ended, only that I felt the reassurance that everything was going to be okay. The next thing I remember I was getting up, going out the door into the lounge. I felt protected and the anxiety disappeared. I finally got the reassurance I needed. Without that reassurance I would not be alive today. That moment gave me enough hope and courage to say 'okay let's go ahead and try.' Probably at that moment, I decided I'm not going back to booze or pills and I'd rely on God. That was the beginning of my true sobriety."

Only after Bob let himself be held like an infant could he begin his long journey back to maturity and health. His experience resembled a classic conversion more than those of the other men. Bob had found a new consciousness. He clearly identified the someone holding the baby and him as God. That day dramatically marked the beginning of nearly twenty years of sobriety.

Carl Jung believed that hopeless alcoholics could only recover through "vital spiritual experiences [when] ideas, emotions, and attitudes which were once the guiding forces of the lives of these men are suddenly cast to one side, and a completely new set of conceptions and motives begin to dominate them."

Though many people today recover from alcoholism through regular attendance at Alcoholics Anonymous and not solely from "vital spiritual experiences," Bob was one of the fortunate ones. In a single moment he "cast to one side" the destruction of his life and adopted a new way of living without drugs or alcohol. Though this spiritual awakening in no way made his new life easy, his hope was restored for the first time since he could remember. The moment opened a window in his soul that gave Bob a glimpse of a world free of terror — just a glimpse, a brief moment, no more than "a second or ten minutes." But it was all he needed to begin to undertake the real task of becoming human, becoming a man among other men. The sacred moment was a gift which liberated Bob "to undertake the hard work."

When he was discharged from the hospital, he voluntarily admitted himself to a halfway house for recovering alcoholics. Through the halfway house he got a job sweeping floors for minimum wage and later another job as a pest exterminator. Eventually, he and his wife attended a Des Moines area community college and got associate arts degrees in drug and alcohol counseling. They both became counselors for the Alcoholism Center in Ames, Iowa.

As he regained his self-esteem and confidence, Bob eventually returned to his data processing training and got a job as a technical analyst, which he has done for the last fourteen years. His own spiritual security became a priority. Bob never again took a drug or drank alcohol, nor was he hospitalized for emotional problems. His wife went on to become a social worker, and they have been married for thirty years.

Though Bob owed his life and sobriety to his sacred moment, he kept silent about it for years. What was it in Bob that kept him silent about such a critical event in his life? Wouldn't it have been quite natural for him to talk to his wife or a close friend?

"I wasn't sure how people were going to take it. It's a personal type of thing, an intimate moment," he said. But wasn't an intimate moment just what Bob might share with his close friends and spouse? What did his inability to talk openly with his wife say about his relationship? What did the secrecy say about his isolation from those he regard as friends?

"People will think you're a little goofy or they're liable to say you're wacko," he added. Certainly Bob's addiction and hospitalization gave him more reasons to fear being called goofy than his sacred moment. The sacred moment had saved his life! How could a close friend or spouse find the dramatic change in his behavior more goofy than his starting each morning with a Mickey Finn? Bob did say that if someone regarded his sacred moment as hallucinatory, he was convinced that "the experience wasn't the same as the experiences I had on my medication."

Five years later, Bob finally talked about his experience at an open meeting of Alcoholics Anonymous. His wife was in the audience that evening and heard her husband's story for the first time. It wasn't until he got some self-confidence to share that kind of experience was he able to discuss the moment openly. Then, Bob found self-confidence and trust in himself to reveal not only his sacred moment, but the defeat, the humiliation, and the ashes out of which the experience arose. Finally, Bob could admit it not only to his fellow recovering alcoholics and acquaintances, but to his wife.

He spoke about how his spirituality had changed from what it was like before his spiritual awakening. "For a long time there was a God worshipped in church and the personal God I found in the AA program. I didn't find a personal relationship with God in church. Later, I found a relationship with a Power greater than myself that worked and kept me sober. For some reason, that was not the same God I tried to find in Church.

"I no longer have to have a mental image of what I believe in. God reveals Himself to me in different ways. If I try to define what I believe, I'll limit it and I don't want it to be closed. God is personal, present, not theoretical, but a 'comedian playing to an audience that is afraid to laugh.' God has a sense of humor."

Bob did not feel more special or holy than other men. "I'm still struggling like a lot of other people. What I've got to offer is what I've been through. I sure don't claim to have any answers, but for the first time in my life, I'm okay with me. Sometimes I can feel the peace right here in my chest where the knot used to be. It's a beautiful feeling of absolute peace. Sometimes I'm filled with this peace.

"As far as I'm concerned, the person I used to be died in Mount Pleasant in 1972." Only then did the sign 'Absolutely No Drugs or Alcohol beyond This Point' take on a new, more pervasive, meaning for him. 'This Point' became his sacred moment when Bob believed God had given him a second chance to live.

Nearly twenty years later, Bob recalled the bargain he made with God to help other people. His belief that he was given a second chance is the keystone to his spirituality. His promise or bargain wasn't something he fulfilled only on Sundays at a Methodist church he attended regularly. It is an ongoing task that requires daily attention. "I do the best I can to help other people, which is the commitment I made to God in the first place," he said.

Today, he occasionally speaks at AA meetings about his sacred moment in his room at the state institution. He makes himself available to newcomers after the meetings, believing that perhaps a suffering individual in the audience that evening found refuge in his story. After his talk, he mingles in the crowds, shaking hands and welcoming strangers. "I think I was given a second chance to talk to a second person," he said. The sincerity of his commitment to others is manifested when he adds, "but I don't know whether I've talked to that person yet or not."

(

CHAPTER 9

God's Shadow

Work of the eyes is done, Now go and do heart work.

— Rainer Maria Rilke

In 1984, from May through August, I spent the first hour of each morning sitting in a rocking chair in front of the bay windows in my study drinking a cup of coffee. Outside, the neighbor's elm tree formed a green circle of leaves and the flower garden bloomed with red and white tulips in early May. Often a cool breeze blew in through the window and I'd lift my bare feet onto the sill as I sipped coffee and slowly awakened. In that second floor room, I started every morning of those four months in a kind of reverie.

After coffee, I'd take my meditation book from a nearby stand and carefully read the entry for that day. Often I'd close the book and look outside, beyond the rooftops and trees, toward the horizon. Those mornings of contemplation were inner dialogues with my deceased father who died from a massive stroke and heart attack five years earlier when I was thirty-two.

Having recently become a father myself, I thought a great deal about him then. I had many lingering resentments and feelings of guilt. During the last years of his life I rarely talked to him. I often forgot to send him birthday cards. My relationship with him wasn't hostile, but nearly nonexistent. Early in May, I had decided that each morning I would meditate on my relationship with him until I could reach some resolve. I naively hoped for some inner announcement that all was well between my father and me.

While gazing out the window into my past I'd visualize childhood scenes, seeing myself at ten years old again, pushing open the screen door to our house. Even in my study, I could still hear Father yell, "Don't slam the door" just as it slammed shut behind me and I raced outside to play.

I saw myself sitting in the front seat of the car as Father and I drove down E. 136th Street to St. Timothy's Church. Each morning, we attended 6:30 Mass while the rest of the family slept at home. He was a devout Catholic, and I served as altar boy at many of those early morning masses, wearing a white surplice and a black cassock. Its hem often caught on my heels as I knelt at the altar during service. Each time I rose to get the cruets or move the Bible from one side of the altar to the other, I'd tug on my cassock to free it. At communion I held the polished silver paten under my father's chin as he lifted his head back to receive the host. The sight of the Windsor knot in his tie, his double chin, and the thick red tongue on which the priest laid the host made me shiver. His body seemed so real and powerful.

After church Father and I stopped at the neighborhood bakery to buy jelly donuts, sweet rolls, and *kolaches*, his favorite Czechoslovakian pastry. At home the two of us read the paper and ate rolls and cereal. Though we rarely talked to each other at the table, the fifteen minutes we had alone before my brothers and sisters awoke were precious. Often, as he held the newspaper in front of his face, I'd lean across the table and read the backside. If he started to fold the paper over, he'd wait for me to finish reading a sentence if I asked him to. I could have asked for anything then and would have gotten it.

My father was a giant like fathers were supposed to be for their children. A good man, he took me, my four brothers, and our three sisters sledding, ice skating, swimming, to baseball games, the circus, movies, church, everywhere. My father showed us the world in all its glory. He drove us to school on rainy days and picked us up at lunch time. He bought us new shoes, baseball bats and gloves, toys and birthday presents. During my childhood it was my father, not my mother, whom I remember as the most loving and involved parent.

Months before I turned twelve, my older sister died. She had been sick for over four years with a brain and spinal tumor—cancer. Nothing would ever be the same. Father became remote. He no longer took me places as he once did. Though he was never very talkative, he now seemed to brood more, as well as argue more with my mother. My sister was his second child to die. When he was a young man his first wife gave birth a year after they were married. My father was sitting in the hospital room with her and the infant when they both died quietly in their sleep.

In my study I recalled an afternoon when I was thirteen. I had come home from school for lunch. Both of my parents sat at the table with me, which was unusual then. Their faces said, "We have something to tell you" long before they spoke. I was sipping from a glass of milk, peering suspiciously over its rim at them when they announced their intention to send me to a Catholic military boarding school taught by Irish Christian Brothers in upstate New York. I was stunned and heard only snippets of conversation like "excellent education . . . moral training . . . college . . . West Point. . . ." Weeks earlier, I had discussed plans with my parents to attend a nearby Catholic high school where many of my friends were going. I felt betrayed and shouted no, I wouldn't go away to school. I threatened to run away or not to study, but my threats wouldn't change their minds.

I never did run away, and I studied hard those four years at boarding school. But during my adolescence at military school, my father, who was once a giant, began to shrivel up, shrink, and appear as a dwarf in my eyes. When he came to visit me at school I felt embarrassed around him. Though a grown man, he became a small person, like Snow White's Dopey, and I could no longer speak with him on any serious intellectual level. Though my adolescent arrogance was the primary cause of the trouble, the alienation continued into my adulthood.

In the middle of my last year at school I refused the recommendation I had from a congressman to attend West Point after graduation. My father was undoubtedly disappointed, though he never spoke to me about it.

When I returned home at eighteen, I was hostile, not only to my parents but also to the Catholic Church. My father and I differed not only on religion but on appropriate masculine values and behavior. He believed that military school training, combined with religious instruction, would lead me not only to West Point and a stellar career but also to being an exemplary man among men. His efforts to shape me into a moral and disciplined man backfired when I opposed the military, the Vietnam war, and the Church.

During the late sixties, like many other young men then, I grew my hair long, and in college I took English and psychology classes, kept a journal, wrote poetry, and led an unconventional life which further alienated me from my father. He remained religiously devout and conventional as I took up the banner of sixties radicalism. Though our philosophies were remarkably different, we didn't argue. That was the problem. We had little, if any, significant communication to the day he died.

After he died, I became resentful that he never spoke to me as an adult or shared his life. He never talked about his relationship with my mother, and I resented that because later my own relationships with women were troubling. Nor did he ever speak to me about the illness and the death of my eighteen-year-old sister from cancer. This became a significant resentment for me because his silence inhibited my own resolution of her death. My own daughter became chronically ill, and I resented him further for not giving me some wisdom to rely on. He had so much to say. Of course, the problem was not entirely his silence but also my inability to listen, to ask the right questions and show genuine interest. But I hadn't understood that and blamed him for my own failures and worries.

My father never recovered from the deaths of his two children and first wife. His silence strangely angered me and affected my life. In a way, I inherited my father's grief like any son might inherit his father's business—in this case his unfinished business.

I distinctly remember the morning I ended my ritual of meditation. It had begun as all the others; I sat drinking coffee, reading my meditation book, and contemplating my relationship with my father in front of the windows. I reached an impasse and couldn't see how our relationship would ever be resolved. I had made progress, but something inside, a gut feeling of resolution, was missing.

That morning I put aside my book, took a last sip from the cup, and swiveled my chair away from the windows. I stood and said out loud in the room, as if talking to someone, "Dad, I think you've forgiven me, and I've forgiven you. I don't know what else can be done."

I paused at the door before leaving the room. I find it hard to admit now what I said to myself as I left because it revealed a certain childishness about me. I whispered, "Dad, God, give me a sign so I know our relationship is healed."

It was a childish plea and spiritually immature to require signs from God or the dead. It indicated a lack of mature faith and trust, and a conflict between what I felt obliged to believe and what I wanted to believe. Still, I did what I did. I desperately wanted a sign to signal the completion of the four-month-long ritual of meditation, but I left the room unsure and walked along the hallway to the top of the stairs. I figured that morning would be the last time I'd sit thinking about my father with such a single purpose. A week later, in order to make room for a desk in my study, I moved the chair to the attic. I put the meditation book in a drawer and never brought it out again.

A year later, on an August afternoon, I was downtown at the public library. I spent a good hour locating, scanning, and selecting some books I needed. With the books under my arm, I opened the door to leave.

As I stepped out into the sunlight I smelled cigar smoke. I stopped and looked to see where it was coming from, but saw no one. I was about to shrug, dismiss it and walk down the stone stairs, but I found myself whispering, "Wait, stop now." Though it was me who whispered, the words gave me the eerie sense that it was someone else whispering.

I stood at the top of the stairs. Suddenly, I realized the smoke smelled exactly like the El Producto cigars my father smoked at home when I was a child. Then it was a constant source of conflict because it sickened me. How many times I whined and nagged my father to put out his cigar while we drove to church. But outside the library I found the smell strangely aromatic and refreshing. Though no one was in sight, the smell in the open air was pervasive, as if someone were smoking right alongside me. I felt a presence that I identified as my father.

I was immediately overwhelmed with gratitude and love for him, feeling a closeness to him that I had never experienced. For me, the effect of the experience was so deep and lasting that I regard the moment as sacred, a gift, a revelation based on an awareness that I had never before experienced.

Less than a minute after I first opened the library door and smelled the smoke, I walked down the stairs saying to myself, "Remember this." This mental note quickly scribbled on the margin of my consciousness has served as a reminder to draw on that experience for reassurance again and again. I had inadvertently made the moment more accessible by not letting it sink into oblivion by the weight of secrecy or self-doubt.

The intense connection to my father was broken and the smell vanished. All that day I felt closeness and love for my father. Whenever I recall that moment, a shiver will go up my spine. Today, if I whiff cigar smoke in an elevator or a foyer I'm immediately flooded with affection for him. It's strange how the smell, which was once pungent and sickening, now signals his loving presence.

Though my reverie that afternoon was brief, the effect was enduring in that my relationship to my father was resolved. In a single moment I had found him when months of hard work brought me nothing. I wanted a sign of healing and my wish came true. I wouldn't say that God stepped off his celestial throne to stoop down for a second and whisper in my ear, "Wait, you wanted a sign and here it is!" Whether it was my father or God above whispering in my ear or a voice from below in my unconscious didn't matter. The experience was spiritual not because of its origin, but because of its lasting meaning. In those few seconds my relationship with my father was healed. I could not accomplish that on my own. I had tried daily for months, but had gotten nowhere. Then in a flash, it was done. I opened myself to the moment, brought myself to the door of that experience, but I didn't open that door. I didn't will the experience into being.

Ever since, my estimation and regard for my father has grown, enlarging him. I enjoyed thinking of him as growing. Of course, I was the one who was growing, but the image of my father getting larger appealed to me in a pleasantly odd way because it allowed me to think of us both growing simultaneously. After the experience on the steps of the library, and another one later, my father grew to size of the Father I knew as a child. It was like time-travel. Both as a child and an adult, I had returned to my youth and to my father.

In 1987, I became seriously ill with Crohn's disease. In September, I had the first of four hospitalizations and four surgeries. I would spend nearly five months in the hospital and months at home in bed. During one episode, my bowel obstructed, perforated, and caused a lung infection. I was put on a respirator in Intensive Care. My family was notified of my critical condition and flew to be with me.

I lay in another dimension of the world that hummed and bleeped with the sounds of the respirator and other machines. I was aware of a friend sitting at my bedside, only she faded in and out of my consciousness with the other people and objects in the room. I was awake and staring at the opposite wall when suddenly my deceased father and sister appeared, standing at the foot of my bed. He was wearing blue trousers, a white shirt with the collar unbuttoned, and his sleeves rolled up to give him a casual, relaxed manner. She wore the yellow night-gown with a white lace collar I remembered her wearing often when she was sick at home. She seemed less casual, more stoic, as if poised as an exemplary model of someone whom illness had not defeated. Father said, "If you cross over, we will meet you." I knew that to cross over meant to die, and immediately I felt at peace with whatever outcome might occur. I was safe, whether I lived or died.

I turned to my friend and whispered, "Look." She glanced toward the direction I signalled with my eyes, but said nothing. "Do you see them?" I mumbled. Realizing she hadn't, I glanced back to where they were standing, but they were gone. He appeared a second time, only without my sister. Again, he spoke and reassured me that if I did cross over he would meet me.

Nurses and doctors often attribute the reported visions of critically ill patients to a kind of temporary psychosis. Supposedly the combination of medication, the intense pain, and the rhythmic, monotonous sounds of life-sustaining machines induce a temporary psychosis which account for hallucinations. Though I was on Demerol and later on morphine for pain, the visions of my father were quite different from the hallucinations I had on my medications. Like Bob in the previous chapter, I would say there was a qualitative difference between the hallucinations I had and the visions of my family members. When I awoke from the hallucinations, I realized their delirious nature. When a friend or a nurse oriented me to where I was, I didn't feel annoyed as I did when my friend couldn't see my father and sister. In fact, I was relieved. The hallucinations meant nothing to me and I was always glad to awaken from them. They were like dreams that came and went. I could hardly recall them, unlike the vision of my father and sister. My father came to my bedside twice, but not one hallucination ever repeated itself or held any lasting meaning.

Some of the effects of the sacred moment were instantaneous and others were slow to come about. Before my illness I considered the concept of heaven or an afterlife as simply one without any basis of sensible experience, but after my near-death experience I knew. It was not a question of faith, but of knowledge and experience. I could say with Carl Jung when he was once asked if he believed in God, "I don't believe, I know." In the same way, I knew there was an afterlife, a life for which I could assert very little. Like many of the men interviewed for this book, I felt no compulsion to convince anyone else. In fact, I didn't wish that knowledge on anyone if it had to be gotten through near-death experiences. My sacred moment proved nothing for anyone else. To argue that it did distracted me from something more important—the meaning of the moment.

Two weeks after the lung infection, I went into shock from septicemia, and my chances of survival grew even more dim. Once again family members had to return to my city.

One day or one night, I floated up above my bed into a doorless white room that had only one window with its shade pulled. While most white rooms make people shudder with thoughts of isolation and deprivation, my white room was brilliant, soothing, and magical. Never in my life had I experienced such a brilliant whiteness before. Any comparison to things like ivory, milk, or alabaster seemed inadequate.

In the white room, I experienced immense knowledge and wisdom. Questions were answered as I thought them. The size of the room varied, depending on what I needed. If I wanted security, the room became smaller and I experienced sensations of being wrapped in something like a blanket. If I wanted expansiveness, the room became a valley. I went to this room three times, and each time I tried to lift the shade on the only window. It wasn't curiosity that motivated me to lift it because I was at peace and needed nothing. Still, I would reach for the shade, and just as I touched it I was suddenly back in the hospital where a visitor sat in a chair alongside my bed. Had I lifted the window shade I believe the final truth—death—would have been revealed.

I always recognized the visitor and knew where I was. Yet I was not the same person anymore. The immediate effect of the sacred room was a new freedom. "Now I can do whatever I want," I said. "I can go anywhere. To Belfast, Nicaragua, Bangladesh, or Lebanon." My announcement must have puzzled my visitor, since she knew I couldn't even turn over in bed by myself, let alone travel to warring and poverty-stricken countries. But I felt exalted with my knowledge and freedom, and the countries I named revealed the sense of a mission and service I felt called to. Though I hadn't told her about the white room, I talked on about my freedom to travel and work, though it would be months before I could even walk around the block.

The first experience in the hospital, seeing my father and sister, convinced me of the importance of love. The moment in the white room revealed two other fundamental values: knowledge and service (or work). Love, knowledge, and service became more than a catchall phrase but three words that evoke powerful moments in my life to this day. My sacred moments, which probably lasted only minutes, convinced me of these truths.

When I left the hospital my abdomen was not stitched closed, but left open to drain. The thick abdominal skin was rolled back to reveal moist, red viscera. The wound was large enough to lay my hand inside and required the insertion of Q-tips four inches into my body to clean pockets. For over a year I changed its dressings and gauzes three to five times a day. Another surgery later reconnected the intestine and closed the wound. I weighed 105 pounds. My recovery would take nearly three years.

During those years I was so disabled at times that I couldn't even walk around the block, let alone open a door to leave the house. For a while I swallowed thirty-two pills each day. Because of arthritic pain and cramping, I often couldn't hold a pen long enough to write a check. I hadn't the strength to open a milk container, sit in a chair for more than fifteen minutes, or stoop to tie my own shoelaces. Early in my recovery, my sister helped me dress myself, which included putting on my underwear.

As debilitated as I was, during those three years I won two writing fellowships, enrolled in graduate school and completed two years with high honors, enrolled for a second Master's degree, coauthored a book published by a major publishing house, signed a contract for a second book, wrote and published other writings about chronic illness and disability, and won numerous academic and artistic awards. I also began my volunteer work for a hospice program and an oncology unit at a local hospital.

I don't list these accomplishments to boast but to illustrate the meaning and effects of my sacred moments, as well as my experience of illness. I accomplished more in those three years than in any time in my life when I was healthy. I was buoyed by a will to live and a strength that certainly wasn't my own. Because of the moments with my father and sister, and my commitment to love, knowledge, and service derived from my near-death experiences, I found the motivation to do what I always wanted but hadn't the commitment to do.

I must emphasize that sacred moments do not make illness and its humiliation any less intense. Often I felt defeated, hopeless, even suicidal. Though surviving illness itself can be a spiritual experience, near-death experiences such as mine in no way lessen one's suffering. It was friends, family, and the meaning that I gave to my experiences that combined to pull me through, not some intrinsic value to being sick. Nothing makes suffering worthwhile. The horror of illness does not always lead to resurrection and health. Recovery from illness doesn't make suffering any more acceptable.

The moments outside the library and in the hospital did help me establish an ongoing loving relationship with my dead father. They reawakened the love I once had for him. Now the child in me loved him, and once again my father was large, like a god, though I pictured him as entirely human and earthy. Even when I reconsidered my father's shortcomings, his silence and emotional distance, every insight I had about him expanded him beyond that memory like an arrow that hit the target but immediately revealed another target that was missed.

One day I realized I wasn't thinking just about my father but about God. For me, every insight into God expanded God beyond that insight. Each vision of God required greater vision from me. God was always larger than I realized. That was why I always liked Tillich's concept of a God beyond God. There was always another God behind the God I understood. As I got closer to grasping Him, He got larger and moved beyond my grasp, not in a frustrating way, but in a way that gave me greater reverence for life, my father, my own body, nature, everyone I knew.

I began to understand the appearance of my father in the hospital and his presence outside the library as shadows of a much larger, illuminating presence. My father was a shadow that testified to another substance, to an afterlife that God cast before me when I was close to dying. On one level my father's presence was very real, and on another level I knew he was a shadow of an unimaginable illumination. In a way, my father led me ultimately back to God Himself. What more could one ask of his own father!

While I was writing this book, my mother died. For months afterward, nothing could make her death acceptable to me. In my mind she did not rise into a heaven or float about in the afterlife where she observed me from on high. Not even the letter she left encouraging her children to rejoice because she was now "in God's Hands" relieved me. She existed in the land of nowhere, in a limbo for the inconsolable.

One afternoon, feeling depressed, I had taken a walk and stopped at the cathedral near my house. For the last few years my only regular involvement with any church had rested precisely in this routine of taking walks and stopping at the cathedral. Few people were there during the afternoon, and I enjoyed the quiet and solitude. The rose windows, the candles, the gray stone and gold cornices, the shrine of saints, and marble communion rail all appealed to my Catholic imagination of the sacred. Though I rarely went to church on Sundays, my visits in the afternoon were frequent, sometimes three or four times a week. I would stop at two side altars to pray. Though I've never felt I knew how to pray, today I believe my desire to pray was a prayer.

That afternoon I stopped at a side altar and considered lighting a votive candle for my mother. She would appreciate the gesture, but the thought of lighting a candle to please her suddenly embarrassed me. How ridiculous, I thought as I deposited a quarter in the offering box. I never did anything traditionally religious for my parents when they were alive. Why now? Wasn't I being sentimental, or worse, hypocritical? As I knelt at the altar's prie-dieu, the inner dialogue arguing for and against lighting the candle continued as if two distinct people were quarrelling inside my head. The conclusion was an illumination for me.

Yes, it was guilt that initially motivated me to light the candle, but I could let the flame burn and put aside the guilt. Kneeling before the statue of Mary, I realized that my mother was now consumed into the Mother God. Suddenly, she was no longer in the land of nowhere, but had joined my father and sister in the Godhead. They were not God, but they were a part of God. The illumination behind my father and sister now was behind my mother as well. They stood between me and the Source, casting one shadow, God's shadow, into my life. The candle was lit for her, but now burned for God.

Sometimes, while grocery shopping, sitting on the front porch or on the couch, I feel the shadow fall over me unexpectedly and I shudder with reverence. It is often a deep, palpable feeling. I may be reaching into my pockets for money to pay the grocer or turning a page of the newspaper on the porch, but I stop and look around me for a darkening of shadow. I don't expect to find any, but it's my way of acknowledging something beyond my ability to comprehend and articulate other than through imagery.

When I left the cathedral that afternoon I felt excited. Now, I thought, I could once again perform the rituals I learned as a child because they were no longer associated with obedience to my parents or church authorities. The rituals could be willingly and consciously performed to express and make visible a private and deeper meaning. The candle probably burned in the cathedral until the janitor came along and with a huff blew them all out. There, the flame in the red holder flickered for just a few hours, but here in my heart it still burns.

CHAPTER 10

Qualities of the Sacred Moment

For lack of attention a thousand forms of loveliness elude us every day.

— Evelyn Underhill

A scientist might explain the biology of a blossoming flower, but that explanation doesn't distinguish why one man, seeing the blossom, shudders with awe and reverence while another sees the flower and shrugs. The difference between a shudder and a shrug depends on the meaning each man gives to the flower. One perceives the holy within the biological, the extraordinary beauty within the mundane, and the other only the rational appearance of the flower.

No two spiritual illuminations are the same, nor do they often occur to several people simultaneously. When Wayne experiences a sacred moment while fishing, his companion may feel nothing as dramatic. Both men are fishing in the same lake but they are spiritually and psychologically in two different boats. Still, sacred moments share certain qualities: brevity, unexpectedness, vivid recall of detail, ordinary settings, ineffability, connection to the Divine or Transcendent Being, and, most importantly, the transforming effect of the sacred.

These qualities are threads that weave the fabric of the sacred moment. They shouldn't be considered exhaustive or applied as requirements. They do not authenticate, but simply describe the typical spiritual experience. Sacred moments are not like UFOs sighted by a group of people in a small town in the Midwest. There is no hotline a person can call to report one. Imagine Jonathan calling an 800 number to report his sacred moment to the Director of Spiritual and Religious Affairs (SARA) in Washington, D.C. The Director himself may fly out to visit Jonathan and inspect his kitchen where he sliced the orange. With federal authority, the Director might rope off the kitchen area and post a warning: *Do Not Enter—Possible Site of a Sacred Moment.*

Perhaps cameramen and reporters from network television might crowd into his apartment to cover the event. They shower him with questions. What kind of proof can you provide to authenticate your experience of God? Did you photograph the orange that revealed the cosmos? The Director might feel horrified to hear that Jonathan ate the orange. If he saved the rind, they will certainly do a lab analysis of it. Afterward, the Director might say, "Sorry. This is just an orange." Or if he is willing to concede the spiritual experience, he might open his briefcase and pull out a sheet with the qualities I discuss in this chapter. He might say, "Hhm, it's brief and vivid. A surprise you can't describe. But you're missing two of the seven qualities." Or he might say, "Sure sounds authentic, but you have no real proof." Of course not. And that is the way it should be. There is finally no proof, no yardstick, that can determine the reality and authenticity of sacred moments.

But I hope men realize that these qualities do connect them to each other in a profound way. Because sacred moments resemble each other in some very striking ways, they indicate a commonality and make clear that ultimately it is not merely an individual experience but a human one.

Brevity

The time that a sacred moment will last is similar to the duration of a dream. Though research in REM (rapid eye movements) can scientifically time the dream state, a dream is nevertheless experienced by the dreamer as timeless. Unless a clock is ticking in someone's dream telling accurate time, a person is not likely to know how long the dream lasted. Sacred moments, like dreams, seem to occur outside of time as we normally experience it. How long it lasts depends on whether it is measured by an outside observer or by the individual experiencing the moment. It is as if there were two clocks, one located on a wall and the other located in the soul. They do not measure the same time.

The men in this book described the duration of their experiences as "less than a minute...ten or fifteen minutes." Many were unsure. When people try to determine the duration of their spiritual experiences they inevitably end up guessing.

Often before we fall asleep, there is a moment when sleep and wakefulness merge to produce an altered state called hypnagogic. During the sacred moment, clock time and "soul-time" also blend the finite and the infinite into one experience, one consciousness, producing a minute that lasts much longer than sixty seconds, and means much more.

To this day I don't have any sense of how long my father and sister stood at the foot of my hospital bed. It could have been a second or an hour. Certainly it didn't ultimately matter. What mattered was that such a brief moment could affect me for so long a time. When I stepped outside the public library and suddenly smelled smoke I felt a closeness to my father that I had never before experienced. Less than a minute transpired from the onset of the experience to the end, but I felt love for my father that has reverberated through my entire life. For all the men I spoke to, the sacred lasts only as long as it needs to to affect them for years.

The men inadvertently discovered the brief but exalted moment when they suddenly felt themselves profoundly moved. They may experience just a touch, as Jonathan did when massaging a man's feet, a fleeting smell of cigar smoke, the first sight of snowflakes in the woods, or a pause in a parking lot before getting into a car. There are many examples in our lives when we briefly glance behind us or out a window and sigh deeply with a sense of peace and well-being. For no particular reason, we may look up from reading the newspaper on our front porches and suddenly remember a toy or an odor from the past and feel grateful. Or we see a man step out of a bus and suddenly we are flooded with fond memories of an old friend. These moments are not all sacred or spiritual experiences, but they are exalted glimpses, sometimes lasting only seconds, that fortify our souls.

How strange it is that such private and brief experiences produce a timelessness that endures for years when other experiences, more public and dramatic, can hardly be remembered. The moments when a judge pronounces us husband and wife, a new employer shakes our hand upon hiring us, or we throw a handful of dirt on a parent's coffin are certainly significant in our lives. We may recall them as vividly as any sacred moment. They may also require significant changes in us. But these moments often become blurred or incorporated into a larger body of experience. Though they have a clear social and psychological meaning that is rarely contested, they are not often experienced as spiritual awakenings.

Unexpectedness

Spiritual experiences occur when we least expect them. We cannot prepare for them as we do for marriages, new employment, or funerals. Though

Greg described feeling apprehensive and anxious as he approached the clearing, he could not anticipate what was going to happen. Nor could I, stepping out of the library, anticipate smelling my father's cigar just outside the door. Months of meditation in my study may have opened me to the experience, but they couldn't produce it. Spiritual experiences always surpass our ability even to imagine them.

Whenever we read about sacred moments, the time always comes when the speaker says, "suddenly." The men in this book often use such words as, "in a flash...at that very moment...just then" to describe the unexpected nature of their sacred moments. Present in each experience of the divine is an element of surprise. The moments are serendipitous in that we discover and experience something we are not seeking, though it may be what we had been longing for. Because a revelation or vision of a heightened reality is unpredictable, we cannot repeat the experience and will feel frustrated in any attempt to do so. Greg spoke of returning to the clearing, hoping to feel the serenity he felt the day before. We can imagine Jonathan cutting another orange on another Sunday morning hoping to experience the unity of all things. I can imagine myself again opening the library door, as I have, hoping to smell the aroma of my father's cigar. Of course we will be disappointed. The experience can't be repeated because it exists beyond the control of human will.

Ignatius of Loyola believed that sacred moments come "without any previous cause....One can prepare oneself for this gift and wait for it, but never cause it." It is always experienced, when it comes, as gratuitous.

No man can decide, "Today, I'm going to have a sacred moment." We can decide to be receptive and open. Though sacred moments are unpredictable, their independence of our desire is "not absolute but relative," as Carl Jung noted. "We can draw closer to them—that much lies within our human reach." And if we can "draw closer," we can also draw away from them. If sacred moments require attentiveness or receptivity, they can be rejected, denied, or minimized.

A rigid attitude toward life may make the experience less likely. The men in this book had to allow a certain amount of spontaneity, even confusion, into their lives to experience the unpredictable. Though stereotypes of men describe them as rigid, inflexible, and controlling, these men are not anything like that. They show a willingness to be moved and inspired much like a man who sets his alarm clock to ring a half hour early in the morning to increase his chances of remembering and experiencing his dreams. We all might set an inner clock so that when it does ring, we awaken and become more conscious of our experiences.

Vivid Recall of Details

All the men recounted their sacred moments as if they happened only yesterday. Because of the intensity, the details can be recalled quite readily. It's as if memory photographs these experiences, and all a man needs to do is turn a mental page to see them again as clearly as they happened.

In each experience of the sacred is the vivid presence of the mundane. We remember how Greg spoke about the size of each snowflake, Larry, the sunlight on his face, Jonathan, the exact slice of the orange, Tom, the pack of cigarettes, and Wayne, the moose and loons. The spiritual experience is constructed of the senses, carried aloft on the wings of the physical. In the midst of these experiences, we become acutely observant and note the smallest detail. Any man might remember the deep richness of the color red in a sunset; he may recall the texture of a shirt, single phrases or words, a particular odor, or the taste of an apple. Often, awareness of these details immediately precedes the experience, which accounts for why some believe the moments are triggered. It's as if God comes to us through our senses, uniting the inner and outer worlds, the spiritual and the sensual, all at once.

William James was convinced that in the realm of religious experience "many persons (how many we cannot tell) possess the objects of their belief, not in the form of conceptions...but rather in form of quasi-sensible realities directly apprehended." Greg's perception of a Presence within the context of sensible data such as the snow illustrates how belief in God is "directly apprehended" through the senses. Partly because sacred moments are always grounded in vivid detail and lively visceral sensations, they seem incontestable to those who have them.

Ascetics and hermits centuries ago emphasized the denial of sense and desire in their quest for God. They tried to purge themselves of all sensuality by wearing hair shirts, pacing in their monastic cells with crosses on their shoulders, fasting, even inflicting wounds on themselves. But sacred moments require equal attention to the ordinary details of our lives. In fact, the sacred always reveals itself in the ordinary. Today if a man is looking for God, he ought to look under his bed, inside his coffee cup, out his bedroom window, or in the attic. If God is indeed within us, then God is embodied.

God's tabernacle is our bodies, fleshy and desiring. We experience the sacred within through our ears, eyes, mouths, hands, and noses. The sacred lies in the ordinary and doesn't depend on human perfection.

According to the poet Rainer Maria Rilke, an angel is not impressed by our great thoughts, profound emotions, and courageous deeds. Angels already know God, the mysteries of the universe, the farthest reaches of man, and are more interested in our ordinary things. It is the texture and sensuality that angels and spirits don't experience. Rilke wrote, "Maybe we're here only to say: house, bridge, well, gate, jug, olive tree, window—at most pillar, tower...show him [the angel] how happy a thing can be, how innocent and ours."

Certainly the men in this book can speak of things in the exalted manner Rilke suggests. They can say, orange, cigar smoke, snowflakes, sunlight, loons, moose. These men can explain to angels "how happy a thing can be, how innocent." The words these men learn to say in a special way reveal that the experience of God always includes bodily sensations. Vivid detail is not only a quality of the sacred moment, but also reveals these men as earthy, and profoundly in touch with the everyday. During their experience, they are not flying above but are, instead, within the world of the senses.

Ordinary Settings

Though there are many exceptions (Duane's experience in the cathedral in San Salvador is one of them), the sacred moment most often occurs in a nonreligious setting. From the examples in this book, we see that it may take place while we are walking through the woods, at our jobs, at a beach, during lunch, at home, on the street, or lying in bed. Though these locations are mundane, the experiences of the sacred seem to enshrine them with radiance, making them memorable and holy. The same goes for places already set aside as religious. The unfinished cathedral in San Salvador is as holy a place as it would ever be for Duane, even without precious paintings and marble statuary, because of the reverence he felt there. Without that reverence, no amount of art, no expenses in decoration, can make it holy. Sacred moments create sacred spaces.

Matthew Fox writes that the kingdom of God is not located at a particular place but rather experienced in body and mind. His emphasis on the individual rather than the place is intended to locate the experience of the Divine within rather than outside a person. Though his emphasis is critically important, it is equally important to stress that the sacred moment does occur somewhere, and all of the men in this book can still, years later, identify the precise spot.

If God is omnipresent as many traditional religions believe, then God is no more in one place than in another, no more evident on one day than another. As Jacob said in Gen., 28:16, "Truly, God is in this place and I never knew it."

Though God may be omnipresent, the experience of God in the world is certainly not commonplace. When we stop at a traffic light in 100 degree temperatures, in a hurry to get home for supper, we may find it quite difficult to believe that God is there too. Then we might agree with Meister Eckhart who wrote, "God is at home in us, but we are abroad." Though the sacred moment occurs in ordinary settings, it is not any easier to experience God in the world than in church.

Ineffability

Though the sacred was vividly and sensuously experienced and recalled, some aspect of these experiences remains ineffable. Some unexplainable sense remains apart from the details and the sensual objects. It cannot be entirely described. Descriptions of this state are often reduced to cliches about our connection to the universe because the experience has no language and escapes every definition. Many of the men felt frustrated when trying to describe their experiences because in essence the experience of the Divine or the Cosmos remains ineffable, hushed, and silent.

During my interviews, I had hoped to hear a common language, words and images that did not degenerate into cliches. I believed that nondenominational men would articulate their experiences in a language void of conventional religious terms and images. I believed men who went to church would have easy access to more traditional religious language to explain their experiences. But the common denominator among the men was not language but the lack of words to articulate their experiences. They definitely didn't speak in tongues, but stuttered, paused, and groped for words. Even more articulate men like Jonathan admitted "it's hard to say." A few of the men seemed annoyed at my persistence and insisted that there weren't any words to describe the experience adequately. They could only compare it to something else by using metaphors.

Use of metaphor and imagery is common in religious texts to articulate the presence of God. It is the use of imagery especially in the Old Testament that makes the Bible so poetic. The texts of saints like John of the Cross, Teresa of Avila, Suso, and many others are abundant and rich with metaphor. The men in this book also employed beautiful metaphors that were not necessarily religious. Wayne referred to a flower blooming inside him. Tom's use of an elaborate analogy to chemistry reminds us of the texts of ancient alchemists. When Bob felt himself cradled like an infant, he experienced the same Motherhood of God as is written in the Old Testament Book of Isaiah 66:13. Jonathan's connection to the universe resembles the traditional mystical marriage to God. The candle burning in my study burns in many sacred books.

Metaphors are frequently used to describe the Divine because they create images that serve to express the ineffable. Metaphor is in the service of intuition, and it is through intuition we most clearly grasp the presence of the Divine. These men possess the same intuitive skills commonly attributed to women. Intuition is not gender-based, but nurtured and developed. When men describe their sacred moment they are not thinking lineally but intuitively as poets. Many of them would no doubt say after reading what I've written, "Yes, but you haven't described my sacred moment exactly." What I haven't explained will remain perfectly clear to them in their bodies where in, Wayne's words, "the flower blossoms."

Connection with the Divine or Something Other

Spiritual moments unite the sky of the mind and the earth of the body, connecting a man to life in a way he had only hoped for. He suddenly finds himself in the midst of unspeakable beauty or heightened reality where he can only stand still in awe and reverence. His ego and ambitions are swept away as he is immersed in a more vivid and fresh understanding of life, the earth, and his relationship to others and to himself.

These moments are spiritual awakenings to something greater than ourselves. We are overwhelmed by a sense of oneness and are at peace. We become a part of a larger reality than we ever experienced, and that reality is a mystery that manifests the Divine. During the sacred moment there is no division of self, no antagonism between the self and the world, self and others, between here and there. We find ourselves united with a deeper self, with a loved one, with God as we experience God.

Fundamentalist religions may object to the

description of God as Something Other. Even more traditional religions may not be tolerant of agnostics like Jonathan or even Wayne who persistently referred to God as "friend," a power greater than himself. It seems to me, however, that the sacred moment is so profound that the word "God" is the only appropriate one. It is justified whether or not the men used it themselves. But for some men, who do not see themselves as religious, the word "God" can be loaded with negative associations. For this reason it's important to define "God" in a manner that will include, not exclude, differences in people's personal faith and understanding of the Divine. If we argue whether these men actually experienced God, we miss the point. We can only be sure that the experience was of Something Other, of something greater than what the man ever imagined.

Perhaps God is only an idea, an archetype, or the ultimate metaphor for human, not divine, experience. We can only know for certain when death opens or closes the door forever to our speculation. But we can be sure that experiences of the Sacred have a lasting effect. As William James wrote, "The only thing that it (the sacred moment) unequivocally testifies to is that we can experience union with something larger than ourselves and in that union find our greatest peace."

Effects of the Sacred Moment

Sacred moments always contain a transformational quality. The transformations recorded here are often spectacular and impressive. Relief from suffering and anxiety was often an immediate benefit of the spiritual. Wounds healed, sometimes quickly but most often slowly. The Sacred did not make the men here supermen, but did strengthen their resolve to live joyously. The sacred moment also had a political or social dimension that transformed them into more loving and concerned citizens of earth.

In the media, the vivid details of sacred moments, like those of near-death experiences, are often sensationalized. In that realm, the Sacred becomes a public spectacle rather than a private event that shapes one's personal faith and commitment to others. This demeans the experience itself. To sensationalize the Sacred inevitably discredits the most important quality of the experience—its lasting and enduring effect. Movies show psychedelic lights and tunnels, relatives seen as eerie ghosts in mists and clouds, and voices that sound like communications from Mars rather than like anyone with whom we spent our childhoods. In this example, the sensational rather than the sacred is emphasized, the origin rather than the meaning of the experience, the past rather than the future that the experience can engender.

It would be an injustice to the men whose stories are told here to focus simply on the drama without a discussion of how their experiences helped shape their spirituality. In fact, the authenticity of these experiences rests in how fruitful they become.

"No one can know what ultimate things are," Jung has written. But we do know from these stories that "ultimate things" can contribute significantly to shaping a man's life. The personal, deeply experienced, expands beyond itself into the collective, and in this way the personal always affects society. Though the experience of the sacred is often kept private for many years, it becomes public for these men in ways we haven't yet entirely realized. One way we have seen resides in the commitment they make to others as a result of their experience.

Each man eventually committed himself to helping others. Bob looks for a newcomer in Alcoholics Anonymous he isn't sure he has met yet. Larry emphasizes the importance of charity and works with other disabled people. Tom counsels troubled young men. Jonathan works with AIDS patients. Wayne counsels the elderly and Greg, younger children. Duane speaks and writes to make others aware of human rights issues in Central America.

Though most of these men kept their experiences secret, it is interesting how they eventually turned to working for others. Their spirituality rests precisely in the transformation of their private experience to a more public one. In this way, each man becomes an invisible pillar in our society, strengthened by his vision of what is ultimately important to him. In a way, they are each Atlas, holding up the world and the globe of the soul. Each man does his share.

Men who showed little self-control before their sacred moment found a new source of strength and courage in giving to others. Larry, whose adolescent ego was his center of gravity, moved the center from the surface of consciousness to a deeper self. These visions do not aggrandize and enlarge the men but rather nurture their appreciation of the everyday. The sacred moment gives each man humility, a proper estimation of his own strengths and short-comings. In the brief moment they experienced the one heart or common soul, they came to know the true size of their own souls.

We've seen how the sacred moment heals wounds, lessens anxieties, and challenges each man to exam-ine his own personal faith. What more can anyone ask from an experience than healing and enlighten-ment? The moment doesn't bring wealth, a leader-ship role in politics or business, or guarantee a posi-tion in a religious hierarchy. Finding God is not likely to make us rich and powerful, affording us with either a new Mercedes Benz or a bishop's miter, but a sacred moment can give us unimaginable peace and certitude.

Through a sacred moment, each man can become more appreciative of the present, of the sensual and physical, more flexible and open to the unexpected, more intuitive and respectful of silences and the ineffable, more religious in the truest sense of the word.

CHAPTER 11

Ultimate and Intimate Concerns

The spiritual life is not a theory; we have to live it.

— Bill Wilson

The brief transcendent experiences of heightened awareness and the ineffable can empower a man to make dramatic changes in his life. Some changes are immediate, while others take years to root themselves. When my deceased father and sister appeared at the foot of my hospital bed, I gained an acceptance of my critical medical condition that I had not had. The change from despair to acceptance seemed almost effortless, but I realize now that I also played a part. I wasn't simply basking on a beach in Transcendental Light. I was a seriously ill man who deliberately availed himself of the benefits of two near-death experiences. I could have waved my hand and said, "Poof! Go away." I could have turned over in bed, questioned my own sanity, dismissed my vision as morphine-induced, and gone on in despair. Then, the moments would have thinned into shadows of memory, leaving me all the more spiritually emaciated.

Another immediate effect was that though I had been agnostic, my sacred moments convinced me of the existence of some kind of afterlife. It wasn't a question of belief and faith but of knowledge and experience. Though I admire men whose faith does not require proof, I was not one of them.

Many of my changes took years to implement and are still evolving. My sacred moments eventually motivated me to volunteer in a hospice, visit the terminally ill at home, read to them, record their last wishes, or simply fix a porch railing for one man who wanted it repaired before he died. I co-facilitate a bereavement group and advocate for people with disabilities. Never in my life had I considered doing these things for others. Eventually, I enrolled in graduate school to pursue a second Master's degree, started a support group for people with chronic illness, stopped worrying about my financial ruin, and delighted in small things like a toy, the texture of a shirt, the buzz of a lawn mower. After my experience in the white room where I understood love as an ultimate value, my relationship with my daughter became paramount, and my new relationship with my father deepened my connection with God.

The changes inspired by my sacred moments and implemented by my efforts are different in many respects from those of the other men I interviewed, but for all of us the meaning of our experience affects three areas of our lives: *the personal, interpersonal, and political/social.*

The Personal

During a sacred moment a man stands, perhaps for the first time, as a whole man, undivided. He is not simply thinking or feeling, but experiencing. Wholeness is as clear as the sun in the sky. The sacred moment takes him to a region of human experience where he is most himself, yet is Everyman. There, the personal and collective become one. The experience expands consciousness and gives serenity. The phenomenon of synesthesia allows him to hear color as music, to experience a taste as a sight. Everything distant is at hand. The universe is not out there, but in our backyards. A simple orange contains the cosmos. Time is not measured in minutes, but experienced as eternal.

Thinking stops being linear and becomes revelatory. The endless chattering of the mind ceases. He hears only the hum of the universe and experiences mystical quietude. Intuition becomes a wing lifting a man up like a bird to see what he could before only guess. Physical sensation inspires certitude. The body is truly a vessel of mysteries. In a sacred moment a man learns more about God than he could in a lifetime of religious instruction. Abstractions like light and truth suddenly have body, smell, and physical life. Joy is a taste, serenity is an apple in a tree, wisdom is our hands, and love is the sound of our name called. The "doors of perception" swing open like church doors and let us out into the sunlight. Questions are answered as they are thought, needs are satisfied as they are felt. Life and death forces coexist like the lamb and the lion. The Garden of Eden is suddenly here, where we have always been.

An experience of this kind can rearrange the very molecules of a man's being and bring into question everything he believes. Imagine being held by God as Bob was! How could anyone go on living the way he had been? A sacred moment turns a man inside out. His boundaries are so broadened beyond what he normally experiences that his psyche seems to belong as much to the world as to his body. For a brief moment, a man slices open an orange and feels instantly welcomed as a guest of the Universe.

Try as he might, a man cannot recapture this feeling of belonging at will. Though now aware of how vast life is, he realizes how little control he has over it. The sacred moment can change his understanding of the world and himself as drastically as a sudden illness or accident. He has no more control over his vision, the experience of wholeness and the divine, than he does over tragic suffering. Both impress upon him his vulnerability and the immensity of life. The sacred moment opens a door into the unknown, the "fear and trembling" described by Kierkegaard, and leaves many questions. What does this experience mean to me? How did it even happen? Why am I so fearful of telling anyone about it? What have I learned? As memorable as the moment is to him, he slowly becomes aware of his own vulnerability and powerlessness. He is not the captain of his ship, but the ship itself, subject to winds, waves, and storms.

I recall sitting in my family doctor's office, hesitant to explain what I meant by my "strange experiences" in the hospital. I was concerned my doctor wouldn't understand, but underneath that concern was the fear of being vulnerable. Fear results when I identify my vulnerability with weakness rather than strength, with the state of being defenseless rather than a primal state of being human. In her office I felt like I was an oyster about to open up to reveal a pearl, but afraid she'd say, "It's a fake!"

I had to stop worrying about what she or anyone would say and accept my vulnerability and mortality. Locking my front door at home every night to protect me from burglars, chaining my bicycle to the telephone pole, or walking every morning to stay healthy may protect me, but these activities don't make me invulnerable. It's important to protect ourselves, but these measures won't give us control over our fate, nor make us impenetrable. We can rig our ships with sails, load our hulls with provisions, carry nautical maps, radios, and compasses, but still there's no guarantee that we will cross our oceans safely. Always vulnerable to a stroke of fate, we depend on merciful winds, compassion from the skies, kindness from fellow travelers, and an eager welcome from friends when we sail into port. The sacred moment compels us to trust.

Since I first spoke to my doctor, the risk in sharing my sacred moments has lessened, not because I am less vulnerable but because I claimed a heartfelt security I first experienced in the hospital. I'm aware now that vulnerability is not something to fear or conceal. It is a state of being that most reveals who I am. How rich sacred moments become for any man ultimately depends on how he responds to his own vulnerability and mortality.

The sacred moment can personally benefit a man in three important ways which will help him more readily accept the human condition. First, *the sacred moment equips a man with ontological security,* giving him a firm ground on which to stand in the world. When a man experiences the Divine or expanded consciousness, he realizes he has always been vulnerable. Afterward he becomes more able and willing to be vulnerable. When my father said to me, "If you cross over, we'll be there," he wasn't giving any guarantees that I would live. He could have just as well said, "Yes, if you don't die today, you will die another day. That fact you can't change, but by accepting it you will be all the stronger." As weak as I was, I felt confident. My father's statement did not deny my human condition, but strangely affirmed it. No matter what happened to me—live or die—I would be okay. This certitude is what men receive from sacred moments.

Vulnerability is a natural state of being that lets the wind blow through the soul, allows uncertainty, even fear, because the sacred moment gives a man an unshakeable sense of who he is, who he's becoming, and who he will never be. No longer in need of pretending to be more or different than he is, he can accept himself. The sacred moment as ballast won't stop a man from sinking, but it will give him resilience. The statement, "Today I may die," helps a man appreciate that, "Today I am alive."

We must remember that the ultimate meaning of the sacred moment depends largely on how willing a man is to be open and take risks. This is not a task for little boys, but mature men with Promethean courage. Herein lies the challenge that each man in this book accepted.

To this challenge men's strength must be applied. Men are accustomed to enduring physical hardships, especially in their work lives. The physical vulnerability they feel in the world of jackhammers and chain saws, on rooftops and oil tanks, is similar to the vulnerability they face within themselves. It requires the same courage men have already shown themselves to possess. Every man must apply these virtues to his inner life as well. With the ontological security of a sacred moment, he can lean his ladder against the home of his soul and climb into the sunlight; he can carry a flashlight down into the mine of his heart.

Experiencing vulnerability does not make a man spineless but stronger. What actually makes a man appear boyish—what Robert Bly calls "soft"—is his failure to claim and assert his humanity. Rather than being empowered by the human condition, he drifts in it like a log in water, swept up and pushed along. This type of man tries to be perfectly understanding and sensitive. He will not raise his voice against anyone, nor pound his fist on the table and say, "No, it's unthinkable!" To be liked is more important than to argue for what he thinks is right. He wants peace at all costs. But a man who is certain about the ground of his being will take risks. The men in this book, conscious of vulnerability, no longer strive to be perfect. They know what Ishmael in *Moby Dick* exclaims, "Heaven have mercy on us all—Presbyterians and Pagans alike—for we are all somehow dreadfully cracked about the head, and sadly need mending." The mature man sees his humanity shining through the crack. He lets go of the ideal and takes hold of the real. He not only admits his mistakes but is willing to risk making new ones. Assertive, he defends his values. His sacred moment will serve as a reminder of a greater reality, allowing him to accept his shortcomings alongside his strengths.

Second, the sacred moment *prioritizes values and gives a man confidence* to be more decisive about his behavior. The men in this book were able to make significant changes in their lives because values were established and clarified as a result of their sacred moments, often creating a new sense of morality. Months after I was released from the hospital, the specter of death was still at hand. I had no time or energy to waste on irritation about trivial things like driving in traffic or running out of stamps. I was glad to be alive, alert to what was truly important.

Universal truths and values made apparent during a sacred moment allow dramatic personal changes to occur. A man may overcome suicidal impulses and seek therapy, find confidence to leave the hospital and begin recovery from alcoholism and drug addiction, make career changes, pursue the arts and vocational interests, volunteer with human service agencies, and do many other things that were unthinkable or impossible before. During my experience in the white room, the values of love, knowledge, and work became so paramount that I was spurred to accomplish more in my career in the succeeding year than I had ever before.

A sacred moment may give a man clarity and confidence to begin new relationships or to end destructive ones, to leave church or begin attending church, to return to school for further education or to drop out of school and resume his original career with more enthusiasm. Whether a man decides to spend an hour a day gardening in his backyard or to become more politically active depends on what values arise as a result of his sacred moment. In either case, the values are lanterns carried through the dark woods of his life, reminding him that somewhere nearby is the path.

Finally, the sacred moment *establishes a starting point in a man's spiritual life.* The sacred moment may be a man's first revelation of God or heightened awareness, or his first step in a spiritual odyssey. Perhaps for the first time he can say, "Now, I have a soul!" The sacred moment can become true north on a man's spiritual compass, pointing him toward a mature spirituality and faith. It can lay the groundwork for anyone to begin his true work.

Like John Newton, author of the well-known hymn "Amazing Grace," who became an abolitionist as a result of his spiritual experience aboard a slaveship he captained, a man may find himself years after a sacred moment writing a song or painting a picture to commemorate the moment his spiritual life began or was significantly deepened.

The Interpersonal

If the only message readers take away from this book is that I'm simply encouraging men to talk about their sacred moments, that would be sufficient. For many, the sacred moment is a secret. To share that moment helps undermine taboos against intimacy as well as those against vulnerability.

What are men really keeping secret when they decide not to tell anyone about their experience? What is Greg keeping from his brothers and father when he chooses not to talk about his moment in the clearing in the woods? What does Bob keep secret from his wife all those years until that day he shares his sacred moment at an open Alcoholics Anonymous meeting?

What these men keep from others is not simply their revelations or visions of God. They are hiding their souls, who they really are, what they most cherish. To reveal a sacred moment to another is like opening our treasure chest. We aren't afraid that someone will steal its bounty, but rather that they'll laugh and say it's worthless. "Spirituality is the most personal thing about you," says Presbyterian minister John Ackerman. It is really the fear of intimacy, not merely ridicule, that most often causes men to keep their sacred moments secret.

What men keep secret are not the facts about unusual experiences in the woods or on fishing boats, but who they are at their most intimate moments. This keeps them at a safe distance from others. They believe it is better to keep the spiritual treasure chest locked up in the attic. By keeping their souls hidden and silent, they deny others and themselves the possibility of further intimacy.

Instead of seeking someone who would understand and help him integrate the meaning into his life, any man can avoid the search for one who accepts and loves him deeply. This search is full of risks and raises issues of trust. Searching itself may be a kind of avoidance—keeping the secret until the perfectly trustworthy one is tracked down, rather than showing the treasure to those who are ready and waiting to admire it. Since Bob could not even trust himself on a walk, one can see how extremely difficult it was for him to trust his wife or a friend with his sacred moment. He could keep at bay the awareness that he had become "like the baby" by blaming others for his silence.

It's no secret that many men are professionals at avoiding intimacy. They have advanced degrees in the tactical logistics of isolation. Men are rarely taught the alphabet of emotion and are kept in a spiritual kindergarten. We learn only that relationships are the business of women, not men. On the other hand, a sacred moment gives a man a lesson in intimacy and vulnerability he will never forget. As a result, he may find himself in profound conflict. Though he knows what it is to be loved by the universe, by all things and creatures, how will he ever find the words and the courage to tell another person?

Though the sacred moment is a soul victory, it also reveals a man's defeats and wounds. This, and not his sacred moment, may be what he keeps silent and secret. In order for Bob, for example, to share with anyone how meaningful and critical his sacred moment was, he would have had to describe how sick he had become. The moment wouldn't have made much sense outside the context of his life experience of drug and alcohol addiction, a troubled marriage, hospitalizations, unemployment, agoraphobia, and childlike helplessness.

Like Bob, many of the men interviewed would have had to admit to their total defeat if they had shared their sacred moment. To admit his defeat to God and himself is one thing, but to admit it to another human being, like his wife, is quite another matter. Telling sacred moments to another involves telling other intimacies. In speaking about their own sacred moments, the men in this book have opened their lives to us. We not only read of Wayne's moment on the oil tank, but learn about his health, family, his son's death, his work, and friendship. Tom couldn't have discussed his experience without revealing his past troubles with depression, juvenile delinquency, his father, diabetes, and the suicide of his ex-wife. Jonathan couldn't have shared his sacred moment without discussing his agnosticism, blindness, and work at an AIDS center. Nor could I have told my own story without telling about my experience with chronic illness. For a man in our society, this admission of vulnerability can be temporarily avoided by keeping silent, by simply saying "no one would understand."

For men, even to talk about spirituality is especially difficult. Though most religious clergy are male, men in the general public are not encouraged or even perceived to be concerned with spiritual issues. It is far more acceptable for women to have a spiritual life than for men, partly because it involves vulnerability and a need for something that one's personal independence does not satisfy. Walk into any church and see who's there. Probably more than two-thirds of the congregation are women.

Greg helps focus the problem, saying, "Having spiritual experiences is not part of the male mystique, a part of society's description of what it is to be a man. Some men have difficulty talking about spiritual experience because they aren't encouraged to express other feelings. If the spiritual experience is not talked about, it is not integrated in your life. Talking about it brings the spiritual experience into the real world. Otherwise it atrophies like a leg in a cast. You cross a threshold when it's shared and communicated, and in the past men were discouraged from crossing that threshold."

It's appropriate to cherish such powerful moments, knowing that sometimes talking about them merely dispels them. Yes, some people will just shrug their shoulders or even laugh. But for many men, silence is a too-familiar response from years of inadequate communication. Comments like "no one would understand," or, "people would laugh or think I'm crazy" should be red flags signalling to men that they are repressing the experience. In these instances, silence is the voice of fear.

If a spiritual experience isn't communicated to someone, even if that someone is only an anonymous other self addressed in a journal, the meaning of the experience can often remain amorphous, undefined, and ineffective. The issues of intimacy and self-revelation never arise. Then such experiences can simply evaporate from memory or be remembered as meaningless curiosities.

Even the holiest of saints, visionaries, and gurus turn to mentors for guidance. For the same reason, it's imperative that a man not isolate himself and instead seek someone with whom he can entrust his sacred moment. A man must be able to say to another, "this is truly who I am in my solitude." The sacred moment can be the occasion for sharing what he has seen in the invisible world and what he tries to make visible in his everyday life.

In *Iron John*, Robert Bly spoke about the need for a man to serve as both mentor and apprentice, to have an older man from whom he can receive counsel and a younger man to whom he can give counsel. Then, a man can find the support he needs to make his sacred moment more efficacious and can lend support to others. Being a mentor and an apprentice offers a kind of check and balance that discourages both repression and self-aggrandizement.

The Social/Political

Much of the earlier excitement and motivation of my experiences in the hospital has worn off, but I am determined now to shape my life along the lines of what was given to me. Sacred moments are gifts, but the gifts are like new clothes. Their true value and beauty is revealed when they are worn and seen, not when they are packed away.

After a sacred moment, a man needs to ask himself what this experience means. It's an opportunity to further reflect on the spiritual meaning of all his experiences. I believe the answer to this question cannot be fully realized unless a man involves himself with the concerns of others. It lies within a man's involvement with his community and its social concerns, as well as in intimacy with another.

When a man experiences what is ultimately godly, he experiences not only his divinity but his humanity. A sacred moment does not put us among angels, but among other men, women, and children. A man's place in the community, as well as the universe, becomes very clear. He now sees how vitally linked he is to others on the earth, as well as to God. He is often moved to strengthen and affirm that link by becoming more socially responsive. Whatever is truly spiritual will always be mirrored in a man's relationship to his neighbor.

Many religious denominations have striven for a social consciousness or a way of putting faith to work in the world. One example of the connection between one's personal faith and the political is apparent today in liberation theology. A major social and political force in Central America, liberation theology creates hope for a Sunday in the future when there will be no difference between God's word and man's word. Churches all over the world nourish grass root movements to help the poor, the sick, and the homeless. Throughout its history, Judaism has been recognized for its social responsibility. The men in this book are no different from the religious in this respect. As a result of their experiences, they have strong consciences. Their personal faith is reflected in their concerns for others, the Earth, and social issues. Greg grappled with moral and political issues raised by the war in Vietnam, as Larry did in managing a house for disabled war veterans in Mexico. Bob and Wayne volunteered to work with people whose lives were afflicted by chemical dependency. Jonathan's revelation increased his consciousness of our planet and ecological issues.

A sacred moment encourages people to become conscious and receptive to creative, global awareness. A sacred moment makes an individual more responsible to others and to the Earth because in his vision or revelation a man will always experience the world as a community. Then, he may be motivated to rediscover the dignity of his work, to make his life more useful through career changes that allow him to deal directly with social issues. A sacred moment can create in a man a heightened awareness of the perils of being male in this society, perhaps enable him to see how victimized he is at physically dangerous jobs, and motivate him to legislate through unions for job safety.

Some of the stories here show how sacred moments can help men heal their relationships with their fathers and in turn become more responsible fathers themselves. One could imagine how poor a parent Bob would have been had he not experienced God as nurturing father, which helped him deal more confidently and responsibly with his alcoholism and drug addiction. Though Bob's growth is personal, we know today that a nurturing father is a major deterrent to violence among boys. Bob makes clear how his personal life is deeply connected to the larger political/social life in which he and all of us are members.

Each of the stories in this book makes clear how the sacred moment can affect a man's life, personally and socially. But all the changes are manifestations of the shift in his spiritual life, which encircles all else.

CHAPTER 12

God-in-the-World

God becomes God the moment when man
becomes man.

— John S. Dunne

Spirituality informs every part of our life. It is the well-spring of experience and interaction in the world. It is illuminated in several ways by a sacred moment.

Most importantly, *the sacred moment reveals God-in-the-World.* In all the stories in this book, God is not a mental abstraction of an invisible Being or King who sits on an ethereal throne. Instead, the Divine is a bodily experience, manifesting a tangible presence in the world. Even the men who recount near-death experiences report vivid details describing the event. Though they may hover near the edge of death while their hearts stop beating, they are still precariously in this world, experiencing a consciousness of life that normally escapes us.

Sacred moments, peak experiences, visions, or revelations of the Divine are always described on the basis of what a man sees, smells, hears, touches, or tastes. Though an element of the sacred moment is ineffable, the Divine—whether it be God or Nirvana —manifests Itself in the sensual. Men not only report a revelatory state of mind, but a heightened experience of the physical. I placed special emphasis on the physical experience of the Divine because the sensual element of spirituality has long been repressed. It is easy for anyone to proclaim that "God is Body and Mind," but difficult for a person to physically experience that unity. In twentieth century American society, we're often trapped inside a labyrinth of thought processes from which we can't escape to experience the simplicity of the Divine in an acorn, a leaf, or a snowflake.

After years of reading about God as Omnipotent, All-Knowing, and Pure Being, it was refreshing to discover men who experienced God in oil fields in Alaska, in the woods, and in traffic. In each story, God is manifested in things, animals, and smells. From these revelations of God-in-the-World, we all can feel a new reverence and respect for this world and the body which has often been ignored in favor of the invisible world of transcendence. The sacred moment reveals the divinity of little things, a white lace collar on a nightgown, an orange, or the smell of a cigar. Truly, the divine does not exclude but includes the world and its minutia.

If, in the beginning, God created the sea and land, the sun, grass, herbs, seeds, fruit trees, and saw that it was good, then only through loving the world and earth do we love and experience God. If a man turns his back on the earth and his world of every-day things, he will not face God in an unadulterated environment. He will face a void empty of children, wind, moon, and leaves.

The path to God may literally be a dirt one, lined with trees, ruts, and wildflowers, or it may be the paved highway we drive, while listening to Mozart on the radio and noticing a glint of sunlight reflected off a car bumper. We've often heard that God is out there, beyond, in the heavens, but the men in this book are speaking about God's presence here, now, and on this earth.

God As Friend

Men who speak of experiencing God as Companion or Friend are not trivializing God as a buddy or pal. We shouldn't misinterpret God as Friend to imply a familiarity that breeds laziness and contempt. Instead, the men are underscoring the original notion of Friend as the one we are free to love. Just as we can lose and renew our friendships, we can lose and renew our friendship with the Divine. By speaking of God as Friend, the men strengthen their love for God in the same way children deepen their love for a parent when they use the word "Dad" or "Daddy," which is what Jesus' term "Abba" means. When one parent is called "Father," some formality and distance is created. When men call God a Friend, they are describing a more intimate God that befits their experience. This is not a debasement or secularization but a genuine effort to make God more present in daily life.

As We Understand God

God may not only be a Friend, but a Father, a Mother, the Enduring, the Earth, or a Power greater than oneself. Whatever one understands or experiences God to be is affirmed by the sacred vision. For many people, the idea of God originates in experiences and dreams. The effort to define God more personally stresses the importance of the individual's understanding of God that is often minimized by impersonal dogma and doctrines. This personal dimension of spiritual experience has often been ignored by mainline churches, yet one's personal faith is the keystone to spirituality.

The personal understanding of God in these stories seems to me more inclusive, more catholic or universal than any single dogma. When a man fashions his own understanding of God he often becomes more tolerant of other religious or spiritual beliefs. In the end, men who work toward committing themselves to the core of a nurturing personal faith will find a "road less travelled" that is vital and engaging.

A Universal Experience

Sacred moments not only nourish the roots of every religion, but nourish many individuals with no religious affiliation. In fact, such experiences have nothing to do with any particular creed or religious affiliation, and they are just as likely to happen to agnostics like Jonathan as to devout religious people. These events do not necessarily convert men like Saul to Christianity, but can and do dramatically change their lives.

Realizing the commonality that is universally shared will help us regard our own experiences more positively. Though the men in this book were certain of the importance and credibility of their experiences, many of them failed to realize how universal such experiences were. As a result, many of them may have felt more isolated by their sacred moments than was necessary. The commonality of such events can help men feel more connected to others with similar spiritual experiences. Sacred moments are not bizarre experiences caused by indigestion and best forgotten, but universal ones that can help shape and direct our spiritual lives.

If we remember that the etymology of the word "religion" is derived from a Latin word meaning "bond" to signify the link between man and God, then we will see the sacred moment as a religious experience in the truest sense of the word. We can put aside the debate concerning the distinction of the words "religious" and "spiritual." Each moment links or creates a bond between a man and the God of his understanding or experience. Today, many people prefer the word "spiritual" to describe that relationship as a way of reaffirming the direct bond. The transcendent experiences of the men in this book not only deepen the meaning of the word "spiritual," but give testament to the origin of the word "religion."

The Light of Life

After he experiences God, a man's everyday world often becomes his church or synagogue. A bond is created not only between the man and the Divine, but between the spiritual and everyday life. Each day of the week is the Sabbath, a day on which he tries, sometimes effortlessly and sometimes painfully, to live his life along the lines of his vision. The sacred moment infuses a man's whole life with spiritual meaning that seeks expression on a daily basis.

The forums for men to discuss their personal piety and faith are few, but a sacred moment makes a man's entire life its forum. At work or at home, among his family or his friends, forums for his transcendent awareness are already in place. If they aren't, the sacred moment creates them, as it did for Bob at a podium during an AA meeting. The experience can create and deepen relationships even with someone long dead.

Once having been linked to God in a sacred moment, each man found himself more motivated to deepen his relationship to the Divine. Though most of the men in this book did not communicate their experiences until many years later, they eventually found guidance and motivation.

Nearly a year after my last hospitalization, and nearly two years after my near-death experiences, I had decided to take my daughter to Disney World in Florida, which Robert Bly described as a place "where there are no ashes." Because of my poor health, I hadn't been able to spend an entire week with my daughter for a long time, so I was looking forward to our trip.

The morning after visiting the amusement center, I was sitting alone outside on the patio which faced a golf course and found myself alienated from a world I found glitzy, sterile, and artificial. While watching suntanned golfers tee off, I suddenly realized that I needed to commit myself further along the lines of the revelations I had in the hospital. Right then and there, sitting in a lounge chair on a sunny morning in March, I decided to volunteer to work in a hospice once I got home. Hospice became my forum. I believed then that working with people who are terminally ill and their families would put my faith into action. I would be among people for whom everything mattered, where "ashes" created substance, where each word spoken is possibly the last, where every detail and gesture is infused with a powerful feeling and meaning that originally forged my own spirituality.

Of course, not every man will choose the same forum for the expression of his spirituality. Because I was unable to work and had time to commit as a volunteer, this avenue was opened to me. I had only to realize it. We've seen how each man in this book chose his own particular way, but it's clear that all facets of men's lives became forums that expressed the meaning of their vision.

His spiritual experience created a need in each man in this book to turn toward others and the community to root his personal faith in a greater collective. The spiritual journey from the private to the public, from the personal to the communal, was sometimes accomplished quickly and sometimes slowly, as with Larry who discovered the meaning of "the prayer in the box" twenty years after his near-fatal experience in the ocean.

Even when taboos against intimacy and vulnerability keep a man's spiritual journey a silent one, sacred moments can still dramatically create or deepen one's spiritual life. What more can anyone ask from an experience than healing, enlightenment, and social conscience? The spiritual experience can deepen a man's relationship to his inner self, leave him with questions that he may have never before asked himself, and positively contribute to making him more complete and whole. The value of a sacred moment should be clear when we see how the experience helps to resolve personal conflicts, commit the individual to the service of others, and deepen his social conscience. By contributing to a wholesomeness of being and allowing a man further intimacy with others as a father, husband, lover, or friend, the sacred moment decidedly and clearly demonstrates its healing.

What do we do then? What kind of practical advice can one give another? After experiencing a sacred moment, where does a man turn to? Perhaps the old story of the enlightened man can shed some light on these questions. When asked what he does now that he's enlightened, the man replied, "I chop wood and carry water." We may have been expecting a more profound answer, but instead the enlightened man states that he simply does his work. Perhaps it is the work he has always been doing. Perhaps he has resumed work he stopped doing during the years he sat meditating or chanting a mantra. When the enlightened man resumes his work he is now a part of his community, doing what needs to be done in his life.

The enlightened man may well be like my neighbor just now, standing outside in a snowdrift up to his waist, shoveling the fine white powder. The cold wind swirls the snow around him as he works, bundled up with a scarf and gloves, his coat collar up around his neck. Shoveling snow is as mundane a task for an enlightened man as one can get. The snow pitched over his shoulder blows back into his face, but surely the enlightened man and the men in this book perform their tasks with an appreciation they never felt before. I believe the enlightened man is aware, perhaps happy, to be working at his task. When he's done, tired and aching, he leans against his shovel with frost on the edge of his scarf around his mouth, delighted by how simple the spiritual life is, how wonderfully ordinary and common is the path, glistening with snow.

How do we know if my neighbor isn't the enlightened man? We don't. The enlightened man wears no halo, nor do any of the men in this book. When the streets are plowed, Wayne will drive his Dodge Colt to work as a counselor along highway 94; Bob will be sitting at his AA meeting; Greg, who has returned to school, will be studying for an exam; Tom, now a stepfather to a rebellious twelve-year-old boy, will probably set a new curfew for his stepson; Jonathan will stand at the bus stop with his white cane on his way to work; Duane will talk on the phone to a client; Larry will finish another page of his autobiography. We all have our tasks, our wood to chop, our water to carry, and our snow to shovel. We are the only ones who know how these tasks resonate in our spiritual lives.

We all need help to live our lives as fully and consciously as possible in order to bring ourselves and loved ones to a wisdom, love, and a "peace that passeth all understanding." But before we can affect our relationships and do our work, we first have to come home to our hearts and souls. Surely, the sacred moment opens the front door.

SELECTED BIBLIOGRAPHY

Achterberg, Jeanne. *Imagery in Healing: Shamanism and Modern Medicine*. Boston: New Science Library, Shambhala, 1985.

Ackerman, John. Personal Interview, 6 January 1993.

Amichai, Yehuda. *Selected Poetry of Yehuda Amichai.* Ed. and Trans. Chana Bloch and Stephen Mitchell. New York: Viking, 1986.

Anonymous. *Alcoholics Anonymous*. New York: Alcoholics Anonymous World Series, 1976.

Becker, Ernest. *The Denial of Death*. New York: Free Press, 1973.

Bly, Robert. *Iron John: A Book about Men*. Redding, Mass.: Addison-Wesley, 1990.

Brown, D. Mackenzie. *Ultimate Concern: Tillich in Dialogue*. New York: Harper & Row, 1965.

Buechner, Frederick. *Telling Secrets*. San Francisco: Harper, 1991.

Campbell, Joseph, and Bill Moyers. *The Power of Myth*. New York: Doubleday, 1988.

Capra, Fritjof. *The Tao of Physics*. New York: Bantam Books, 1977.

Cowan, Marian, and John C. Futrell. *The Spiritual Exercises of St. Ignatius of Loyola*. New York: Le Jacq Publishing, 1982.

Coxhead, Nona. *The Relevance of Bliss: A Contemporary Exploration of Mystic Experience*. New York: St. Martin's Press, 1985.

Dunne, John S. *Time and Myth*. Notre Dame, Ind.: University of Notre Dame Press, 1973.

Fossum, Merle. *Catching Fire: Men Coming Alive in Recovery*. San Francisco: Harper/Hazelden, 1989.

Fox, Matthew. *Breakthrough: Meister Eckhart's Creation Spirituality in New Translation*. New York: Image Books, 1980.

_____. *The Coming of the Cosmic Christ*. San Francisco: Harper & Row, 1988.

Goldberg, Herb. *The New Male*. New York: New American Library, 1979.

Grant, Patrick, ed. *A Dazzling Darkness: An Anthology of Western Mysticism*. Grand Rapids, Mich.: William B. Eerdmans Publishing Co., 1985.

James, William. *The Varieties of Religious Experience*. New York: Macmillan Publishing, 1961.

Julian of Norwich. *Julian of Norwich—Showings*. Trans. Edmund Colledge and James Walsh. New York: Paulist Press, 1978.

Jung, Carl. *The Portable Jung*. Ed. Joseph Campbell. New York: The Viking Press, 1971.

Kurtz, Ernest. *Not-God: A History of Alcoholics Anonymous*. Center City, Minn.: Hazelden, 1979.

Laski, M. *Ecstasy: A Study of Some Secular and Religious Experiences*. New York: Greenwood Press, 1968.

Marty, Martin. *A Cry of Absence*. San Francisco: Harper & Row, 1983.

Maslow, Abraham. *Religions, Values, and Peak-Experiences*. New York: Penguin Books, 1976.

May, Rollo. *Paulus*. Dallas: Saybrook Publishing Co., 1973.

Melville, Herman. *Moby Dick*. New York: Bobbs-Merrill Co., 1964.

Monroe, Robert A. *Journeys Out of The Body*. New York: Anchor Press, 1973.

Moody, Raymond. *The Light Beyond*. New York: Bantam, 1989.

Nelson, James. *The Intimate Connection: Male Sexuality, Masculine Spirituality*. Louisville, Ky.: Westminister/John Knox Press, 1988.

O'Connor, Flannery. "Everything that Rises Must Converge" and "Revelations." *In Becoming Human*. Ed. Richard Dennis and Edwin Moldof. Chicago: Great Books Foundation, 1977.

Osherson, Samuel. *Finding Our Fathers*. New York: Free Press, 1986.

Peck, Scott. *The Different Drummer*. New York: Simon & Schuster/Touchstone, 1988.

Register, Cheri. *Living with Chronic Illness: Days of Patience and Passion*. New York: Free Press, 1987.

_____. Personal interview, 14 August 1992.

Rice, Howard. *Reformed Spirituality.* Louisville, Ky.: Westminister/John Knox Press, 1991.

Rilke, Rainer M. *Duino Elegies and The Sonnets to Orpheus.* Trans. A. Poulin. Boston: Houghton Mifflin Co., 1975.

Ring, Kenneth. *Heading Toward Omega.* New York: Quill, 1984.

Shannon, William H. *Seeking the Face of God.* New York: Crossroad, 1988.

Sinetar, Marsha. *Ordinary People as Monks and Mystics.* New Jersey: Paulist Press, 1986.

Soelle, Dorothee. *The Window of Vulnerability: A Political Spirituality.* Trans. Linda M. Maloney. Minneapolis: Augsburg Fortress Press, 1990.

Solly, Richard, and Roseann Lloyd. *JourneyNotes: Writing for Recovery and Spiritual Growth.* San Francisco: Harper/Hazelden, 1989.

Suso, Henry. *Little Book of Eternal Wisdom.* London: R. and T. Washbourne, 1910.

Tillich, Paul. *The New Being.* New York: Charles Scribner's Sons, 1955.

Underhill, Evelyn. *Modern Guide to the Ancient Quest for the Holy.* Ed. Dana Greene. New York: State University of New York Press, 1988.

Whitehead, Alfred N. *Religion in the Making.* New York: Macmillan Co., 1926.

Zinsser, William, ed. *Spiritual Quests: The Art and Craft of Religious Writing.* Boston: Houghton Mifflin Co., 1988.

Howard Rice — Book. Reformed Spirituality
"believing without belonging"

pg 15 7 qualities of the sacred moment
brevity, unexpectedness, ineffability,
ordinary setting, union with a transcendent Being, vivid recall of details,
enduring transformational effect.
see ch. 8

Shema prayer "Hear O Israel,
Lord our God, The Lord is One."
— placed in mezuza
Mitzza mitzva = good deed
the highest mitzva is giving to a
charity anonymously

pg 80

Other titles of interest...

Touchstones
A Book of Daily Meditations for Men
   Providing practical wisdom and daily encouragement, this popular book opens men to a new awareness of their masculinity, home life, relationships, values, and emotions. Included are reflections on more than 150 topics that offer a place for talking with other men or for daily private meditation. 400 pp.
Order No. 5029

Men in Recovery
Finding Our Direction
   by Merle Fossum
   This illuminating resource examines the special problems men face in coming to terms with their lives. Practical exercises guide men through key life transitions along a path to continual masculine adult development. 193 pp.
Order No. 5041

The Way of Real Wealth
Creating a Future that Is Emotionally Satisfying, Spiritually Fulfilling, and Financially Secure
   by Mark S. Waldman, Ph.D. CFP
   The Way of Real Wealth provides exercises and personal stories to help us recognize the deeply ingrained beliefs we have about money. Author Mark Waldman, the "Money Doctor," leads us to a better awareness of life's potential by viewing money from a spiritual perspective. 224 pp.
Order No. 5050

For price and order information, or a free catalog, please call our Telephone Representatives.

HAZELDEN

1-800-328-0098	**1-612-257-4010**	**1-612-257-1331**
(Toll-Free. U.S., Canada and the Virgin Islands)	(Outside the U.S. and Canada)	(24-Hour FAX)

Pleasant Valley Road • P.O. Box 176 • Center City, MN 55012-0176